THE BALM TO HEAL AMAVUTA YOMORA

A SURVIVOR'S JOURNEY TO EMPOWERMENT

J. B. MANYWA

Copyright © 2025 J. B. Manywa.

All rights reserved. No part of this book may be used or reproduced by any means, graphic, electronic, or mechanical, including photocopying, recording, taping or by any information storage retrieval system without the written permission of the author except in the case of brief quotations embodied in critical articles and reviews.

This book is a work of non-fiction. Unless otherwise noted, the author and the publisher make no explicit guarantees as to the accuracy of the information contained in this book and in some cases, names of people and places have been altered to protect their privacy.

WestBow Press books may be ordered through booksellers or by contacting:

WestBow Press
A Division of Thomas Nelson & Zondervan
1663 Liberty Drive
Bloomington, IN 47403
www.westbowpress.com
844-714-3454

Because of the dynamic nature of the Internet, any web addresses or links contained in this book may have changed since publication and may no longer be valid. The views expressed in this work are solely those of the author and do not necessarily reflect the views of the publisher, and the publisher hereby disclaims any responsibility for them.

Any people depicted in stock imagery provided by Getty Images are models, and such images are being used for illustrative purposes only. Certain stock imagery © Getty Images.

Scripture quotations marked (NIV) are taken from the Holy Bible, NEW INTERNATIONAL VERSION®, NIV® Copyright © 1973, 1978, 1984, 2011 by Biblica, Inc.® Used by permission. All rights reserved worldwide.

Scripture quotations marked (ESV) are from the ESV® Bible (The Holy Bible, English Standard Version®), copyright © 2001 by Crossway, a publishing ministry of Good News Publishers. Used by permission. All rights reserved.

Scripture quotations marked (KJV) are taken from the King James Version, public domain.

ISBN: 979-8-3850-2464-3 (sc)
ISBN: 979-8-3850-2465-0 (e)

Library of Congress Control Number: 2024908953

Print information available on the last page.

WestBow Press rev. date: 02/04/2025

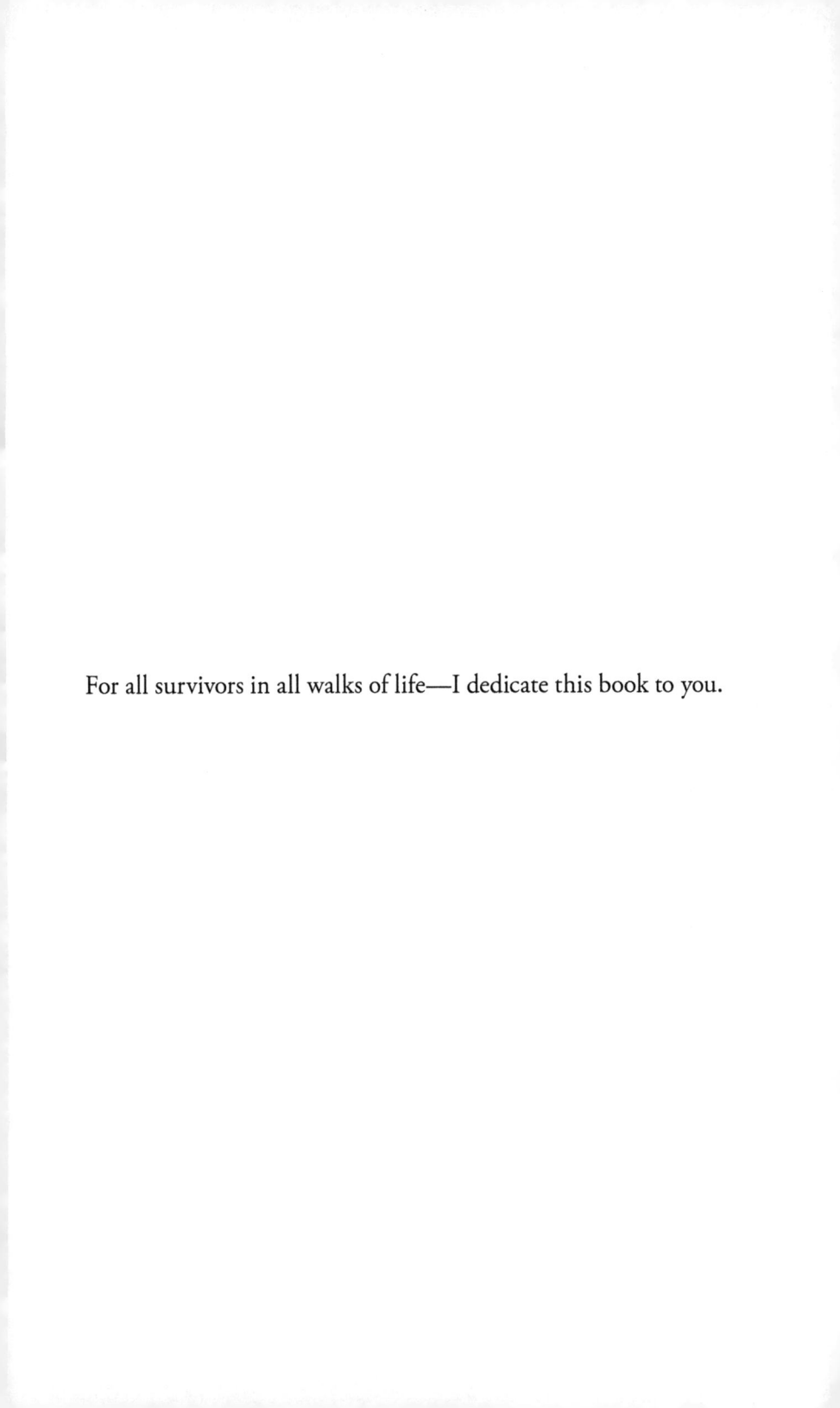

For all survivors in all walks of life—I dedicate this book to you.

CONTENTS

Introduction ix

Chapter 1: Where My Story Begins 1
Chapter 2: Living While Grieving 9
Chapter 3: Starting to Live Again 18
Chapter 4: It Is A New Day! 30
Chapter 5: Find Yourself and Your Vision 42
Chapter 6: Planning and Preparing to Thrive 53
Chapter 7: Manage, Invest, and Enjoy 62

Conclusion 77
Appendix: *My Testimony*: I Barely Survived 81
Acknowledgments 91
About the Author 93

INTRODUCTION

I have a story to tell, a journey to share, and a lesson to give. How I went through fire, how I made it to the other side, and how you can make it through tough times also. As you read this book, you will find out what I have been through; don't worry, it all worked out for the best in the end. It's impossible for me to know how many unfair disadvantages exist in your life, but if you were disadvantaged and have been dealt unfairly with life in some ways, my message to you today is this: don't dwell on what has been taken away from you. Instead, use what you have left to live the best life you can.

Many people have heard about Rwanda and what happened there in 1994. In *The Balm to Heal*, I share some of what happened and my experiences during that unthinkable and inhumane time, known as the Genocide against the Tutsi or the Rwandan Genocide as some call it. Since much has been written and presented in videos and other media about what happened, my plan is not to focus on the details about genocide, but rather to share my journey through it and how I regained my life.

The main thrust of the book is not the tragedy I lived through or how I rebuilt my life. The main point of this book is you, your life, and how you can make it despite all you have been through. You've likely lived through some impossibly challenging times. You may feel drained and hopeless, but you have a future. You can build a thriving life, no matter what you've been through. This book will show you how.

Chapter 1 gives some background about my story and shows how I survived and how you can too. If you're curious about the full story of what I experienced in 1994, you can start with the Appendix.

Chapter 2 highlights the difficulties we face as we emerge from suffering to rebuild our lives.

Chapter 3 shows you concrete ways to take the first steps to a new life.

Chapter 4 invites you to see hope and possibility in the future.

Chapter 5 gives you the tools to craft a vision for your life.

Chapter 6 helps you begin to make your vision a reality.

Chapter 7 shows you how to reap the rewards of your new life.

More than anything else, this book is a gift from me to you. We are two people who have suffered greatly. I share my wisdom and experiences with you, but what I hope to share most is this *icyomoro*, which is a healing balm. I've healed in ways that once seemed impossible, and that's what I want for you. I need you to know that life will continue after what you've been through, and life can be good again.

> For there is hope for a tree,
> If it is cut down, that it will sprout again,
> And that its tender shoots will not cease.
> Though its root may grow old in the earth,
> And its stump may die in the ground,
> Yet at the scent of water, it will bud
> And bring forth branches like a plant (Job 14:7–8 NKJV).

How the Genocide Began

The roots of the genocide are generations deep, but an incident on April 6, 1994, opened the door for the violence the former government had long been planning. The president's plane was shot down near Kigali Airport, killing him and the president of neighboring Burundi. Over the next hundred days, an estimated 500,000–860,000 or more Tutsi were slaughtered, along with the Hutu who did not agree with the government's management of societal problems.

Thank God for the Rwandan Patriotic Front army (RPF) that had disagreed with the policy of dividing Rwandans, and had managed to defeat the government that supported the ideology of genocide. They took control of the country in July 1994.

Once a new government was installed, they recognized that they had inherited a country in shambles. Most of the infrastructure had been destroyed: there were no banks, public transportation, schools, places to shop or buy food, or hospitals to care for the sick. Corpses lay everywhere. Dogs were eating corpses, and the stench of death permeated the air. The first order of business for the new government was to clean the cities, bury the dead with honor, and provide justice.

We were lucky to survive, but we felt like dead men walking. We were existing, but we weren't living. We weren't dead, but we had no ambition, excitement, joy, happiness, or peace. We were barely alive. Yet somehow our sense of hope was restored when the killing stopped. That kept us going.

The country's recovery has been long, complicated, and painful, but there is now a gleam of light and hope in Rwanda. That light may be dim at times for the survivors—and the many other citizens who are trying to make life work after great loss—but the sense of hope there is extraordinarily strong.

The Ditch

During the genocide against the Tutsi in Rwanda in 1994, I was literally buried alive. Only by the grace of God was I able to dig myself out of my grave. I use that experience as the foundation for this book, and hope it can be a source of inspiration that helps you push through any dark times you face.

The ditch I was stuck in was a physical one, and digging myself out was extremely difficult. I have come to realize that digging myself out of the mental and emotional limitations that I was left with after the genocide and war was also hard. In fact, one could even say it was harder, because it lasted a long time compared to surviving the genocide itself. This is a common experience for survivors of life-threatening tragedies.

During that horrible massacre, we were beaten nearly to death and thrown into a septic tank—on top of dead bodies. Eight of the killers lifted a ten-inch-thick cement lid that had previously covered that hole and put it back on. Their idea was to leave us there for seven days. If we did not die of hunger, they would come back and finish us off with stones. Luckily, that did not happen. For that, I thank God.

We were miraculously able to get ourselves out by digging with our hands and a car's shock absorber that had been thrown at us while they were tossing us into the septic tank. It was thrown to wound or kill me, but it ended helping us escape.

What we saw and went through changed our lives forever. Some of the experiences have made us stronger, and others have made us vulnerable, much like when the smoke clears after a fire. I am here to tell you that you can regain your life after almost losing it.

You can dream again and achieve your dreams.

It is okay to hope again, to love again, and to laugh again. No matter what you've suffered, it's okay to live again.

Whoever you are, or wherever you were born, we all were given one life. What makes a difference is how we choose to live it.

CHAPTER 1

WHERE MY STORY BEGINS

It's not about the cards you're dealt, but how you play the hand.

— Randy Pausch, *The Last Lecture*

Let's Start with Thanks

IF YOU CAN BREATHE AND move, laugh and cry, and talk and see—or you don't have much going on—you can be grateful. If you can breathe, you still have a chance. You have a chance to make a change, love again, live again, and enjoy life. That chance is there for the taking if you wish.

For the chances you have, whether small or large, be thankful.

We can choose to be miserable and sad about what went wrong in our lives, but that will not add anything to life. We risk losing even the little we have.

Being thankful is beneficial, especially when you are surrounded with more losses than gains. No matter what your current situation is, there is always something to be grateful for.

> Anyone who is among the living has hope—even a live dog is better off than a dead lion! For the living know that they will die, but the dead know nothing; they have no further reward, and even their name is forgotten (Ecclesiastes 9:4–5 NIV).

I have many reasons to be grateful. I am a survivor of something horrible, inhumane, and rare, but I get a chance to tell my story for you to read. I hope I can inspire you to love life and live the life you love. I hope that will be the case for you after reading this book.

Love to Live Again

One would think that after surviving such atrocities, we would love life, but this was not the case for me. It is certainly not the case for many survivors of genocide, but it is for most of them. Even though we physically survived the tragedy, we were left with a semblance of living. Our actual lives were taken away from us, yet we were still breathing.

Think of it as living with no dreams or ambition, and no ability to handle stress or tackle difficult issues in marriage, raising kids, holding jobs, or running a business.

The past can take so much out of our lives that facing the future seems almost impossible. It is only by grace that I am still alive. I have a feeling that it might be true for you as well, but I can only imagine what you have been through.

No matter what you have been through or how much, I invite you to join me on life's journey. We will figure out how to make sense of what happened to us, and then we can learn how to use it to help us face tomorrow. No matter how horrible the past has been, no one has the power to change it. We can all do something about the future by taking the right steps, starting in the present moment.

Not one human being among us has the power to stop time or

reverse it, but all of us have the power to plan how we are going to face the future. We may not be able to redirect the wind, but we can adjust our sails. The past is the past, and there is nothing we can do to change it. However, we can hope, and we have a chance to change the future.

> When you can't change the direction of the wind, adjust your sails.
>
> —H. Jackson Brown Jr.

My Childhood

I was born and raised in Rwanda. My childhood was beautiful—at least I thought it was. We had food to eat and a place to sleep, and we had each other.

My mom and dad owned a convenience store, and they both sewed on the side to help pay the bills.

In the neighborhood, we played with the other kids. We were oblivious to the country's ethnic issues. Just like most children, we did not know about the politics of our country. There were not that many options for games, but we were creative and had fun. We built cars from grocery boxes and fence wires; we played soccer barefoot and swam in rivers.

At home, we enjoyed what little we had. We started a band and used cooking oil boxes as drums and tiny ropes as strings for guitars on oil steel boxes. We used wood and nails to hold the strings. We even had a kids' theater and used torches as lights. Someone would stand behind the curtain and change the images of different characters drawn on paper. We built homes in mud and slid on banana peels after the rain. We played hide-and-seek, and we imitated adults' weddings and we pretended to cook. Overall, life was beautiful and fun. We were children. It was as simple as that.

However, for my parents, things had not been as they should have been for a long time. Ethnic division and racism had been a threat to their livelihood for their entire lives. The political atmosphere had not been in their favor, and they'd always felt the brunt of it. It wasn't until I was nine or ten years old when I learned that our family was regarded as different in the eyes of the government.

I don't know how familiar you are with the ethnic divisions among the people in the Great Lakes region of the eastern part of Africa, but, in short, during colonial rule, people in Ruanda-Urundi, now called Rwanda-Burundi, were divided into three groups: the Hutus, the Tutsi, and the Twa or Batwas. The colonials made the first group the elites, the second group was the peasants, and the last group was the artisans. This created resentment among the people. The country eventually erupted into political chaos, decades of civil wars, and what is historically known as the genocide against the Tutsi in 1994.

The truth is that whenever the division of people is the goal, there is always a way to achieve it. It is shameful that those baseless divisions have caused the death of hundreds of thousands of people, and that the killing continues. It is disgraceful for the colonials who invented it, and it is shameful for those of us who continue to perpetuate those divisions and keep those distinctions alive to this very day.

The Source of All the Problems

The aftermath of colonialism left a division among the citizens of Rwanda, and some of us reaped evil from that seed. Those groups have different histories, and by the time I was born, the differences were deeply entrenched. No one gave much thought to how or why we were divided. We thought it was just the way things were.

The roots of the division were so deep, but to be fair, part of it was our own doing. It is accurate to say that colonialism facilitated hatred in our part of the world, but what about our contribution to the problem? Why does it continue in some parts of the Great Lakes region after so many years?

War is still taking place in the eastern part of Congo, which borders Rwanda to the west. This affects Uganda as well, which borders Rwanda to the north. Tanzania, which borders Rwanda to the southeast, is currently involved in this war as part of The Southern African Development Community (SADC) organization. SADC is comprised of sixteen member countries and those who are in Congo are part of a joint effort with the UN mandate called MONUSCO, which has been trying to bring peace to that part of the world for more than twenty years. There is also Burundi, which borders Rwanda to the south, and their army is also in Congo.

Due to similarities in culture and history that Burundi and Rwanda share, Burundi's involvement in this conflict can have a more disastrous effect and be very detrimental compared to how this may affect DRC, Uganda or Tanzania. That is because Rwanda and Burundi share numerous similarities in culture, language, and history, more than those other countries. In fact, Burundi used to be referred to as another Rwanda during colonial times as Rwanda-Urundi. If the world does nothing, genocide or something worse could result. For what reason? Power? Resources?

Some say all those wars have erupted in response to the presence of underground minerals, such as gold and diamonds, and political power, but other countries have been blessed with similar riches and the people are not involved in killing one another.

One would think that things would have changed after thirty or more years, and that we would have learned from history, but that is not the case. This time, the worry is not only for Rwandans and the Tutsi; the entire region is being affected. Thousands of civilians have been killed, thousands of women have been raped, and thousands of families are stuck in refugee camps with little or nothing to eat and little or no medical attention. A majority of them have been born in refugee camps, gotten married in refugee camps, and had kids and grandkids in refugee camps. Young people have been forced to join the fight. Some received minimal army training, but others were handed guns and sent to fight—or be killed. There are also trained soldiers on the front lines, but there are also many soldiers and mercenaries from other nations and continents. It is like a world war is taking place in a small region with minimal media attention.

If the past has taught us anything, it's that what affects a group of people on one side of the world can impact those who are nowhere nearby. Right now, it looks like a problem for the people in Congo will become a problem for the world in a few years. We are one family of global citizens, and all hands should be on deck to do something about it. This applies to Congo and to wherever else something like this is happening, regardless of race, color, religion, or place of origin.

Thirty years ago, the entire world closed its eyes and allowed a genocide of the Tutsi in Rwanda to take place. The UN had soldiers protecting people who were targeted and placed them in schools, churches, and even the soccer stadium, which was the headquarters for the peacekeepers. Eventually the peacekeepers left the country, and things escalated. Religious workers from abroad and diplomats from different embassies were evacuated and left the local people to be decimated. Maybe the circumstances were different then. Some tried their best to save people, but most of them failed. Maybe it was impossible then, but what about now?

A New Mind for a Way Forward

After the 1994 massacre in Rwanda and what is now happening in eastern Congo, one can only cry and hope that it is resolved somehow. Countries, including the United States, are encouraging peace talks, but one can only hope.

If other places in the world have valuable commodities and are not killing each other to gain control, it means we can happily live with each other as well.

For that to happen, there is a lot that we need to improve, most importantly our mindset. If we still have people who believe in killing one group of people to create a majority for what is painted to be a democratic vote, our thinking is divisive and weakens us all.

There are always special interests and outside powers that can instigate or support divisions for their own gain, but a person can never deny that they did wrong because someone else made them do it. We all must sit down and be honest with ourselves, so we can own up to our share of the chaos. Taking responsibility is critical in every part of life.

Owning our mistakes and adjusting our mindset can help us dig ourselves out of the deep hole of self-destruction we are in. We mustn't move away from thinking that we are the keepers of our neighbors.

My Testimony

I placed more details about how I survived in the Appendix, but here is what happened in a nutshell:

- The president's plane was shot down on April 6, 1994.
- My parents organized for us to flee our house separate ways.
- The Interahamwe militia went to where most people had fled and started killing them.
- We ran and were able to escape, but we were found. The killers decided to bury us alive and then stone us to death after seven days if were still breathing.
- We were able to dig ourselves out, thanks to two days of nonstop rain, which made it easy to dig around the bricks and concrete.
- We found RPF soldiers who helped us to rejoin other civilians.
- Later on, I was able to migrate to the United States.

Life after the Genocide

Life after the genocide was difficult, to say the least. My mother struggled to take care of us. With few resources, lingering injuries, and grief, she still managed. I used to think she was old then, but when I think of how young she was when she became a widow, I laugh to myself. I can't even understand how she made it through every day. She was able get her convenience store up and running using money from sewing as an initial investment and rent money from a few rental properties my dad had left. She is my hero.

CHAPTER 2

LIVING WHILE GRIEVING

WHAT WE WENT THROUGH DURING the time of darkness caused a lot of pain and left deep scars in our lives, in our hearts, and on our bodies. Some people who lost body parts will never recover physically. Some of the scars are visible, but others are not. Some of the scars healed easily, but others did not. And, some did not heal at all, and all we could do was pick ourselves up and try to move forward. We did the best we could with whatever we were left with.

It took a long time to heal from all I experienced during the genocide. I lost so much and suffered so much. What I saw, I will never forget. I wondered if I'd ever feel alive again. However, I discovered that the bigger issue wasn't so much what had happened to me; it was what I would do about what had happened. The problem is how can we overcome whatever happens to us? Everyone has a story. Some are more horrifying than others, of course, but everyone who has lived only a millisecond has a story. Some people lived to tell their stories, but others did not. Some survivors never overcame the hardships they survived. That was me, for a while, but it doesn't have to be you. Even if it has been you, your future doesn't have to be dictated by the past: "Anyone who is among the living has hope—even a live dog is better off than a dead lion" (Ecclesiastes 9:4 NIV).

The odds of surviving a genocide that took close to a million lives are very slim, especially when you are the target with nowhere to run or hide. Being able to make life work after such a horrifying experience is difficult, but it is possible. Please never lose hope. I survived, and I learned to live again. I want to share with you what I learned so you can live again too.

Imagine waking up one day to face life with most—or maybe even all—of your friends, family members, neighbors, teachers, and schoolmates gone. That's what we faced after the genocide. We were all grieving, and we were all in so much pain. Over time, our sense of hope and our thirst for life came back. Yours will too. The country also recovered. Rwanda is no longer known as a place of mass killings. It is a safe country of hope and recovery, and economically on the right path.

Arsenal Football Club sponsored a campaign called "Visit Rwanda," and the Commonwealth Heads of Government Meeting (CHOGM) was hosted there in 2022. The biennial summit meeting included governmental leaders from all Commonwealth nations, including the current king and queen of England. Considering our nation's past, it is hard to believe. Who would have thought a place that was known for mass killings would be a safe place for people of all nations, and for heads of state? With intentional choices, you can find a way forward, like I did and like Rwanda did. It's worth the effort.

For many months we had to live in a war zone with dead bodies all around us. It was impossible to avoid grim, horrifying reminders of what had happened. We were happy we had survived, and we were grateful to the RPF soldiers who rescued us. We were angry at the government because it had betrayed us, even though we knew we'd be targets. We were disappointed in the international community for abandoning us. Most of all, I was afraid that it would happen again. We had to face life with no strength, no drive, no ambition, no faith, no dreams, and no goals. Basically, we were like dead men walking. It seemed like there was no point in living. It felt like life had no value anymore.

We survived and were happy that we had survived, but we were sad and angry because life made less sense than it did before the genocide.

Before the genocide, I was a good student with very good grades. After the genocide, I could not find a reason to motivate myself to be number one in my class. I had always looked forward to making my father proud, by achieving the highest grades in my class. After the genocide, I lost that drive because he was no longer alive. I thought, *what is the point?*

"Let us eat and drink, for tomorrow we die" (1 Corinthians 15:32). That was the mentality for many of us. It made sense that we felt that way, but that belief hurt us. In that scripture, Paul was wondering about the reason for his struggles. It is extremely hard to strive to fulfill a promise when you know it could vanish at any moment. That is what life seemed like to me. How could anyone convince me that there was value in life after I had experienced the loss of life on an unimaginable level?

It was difficult to break through the limitations I felt after what I had endured. I know that I am not alone; we are still here, which means we can do something about it. Changing how we view our lives will determine how we are going to live it. If your energy is focused on what went wrong and not on what can go right, the healing will be delayed.

Once I changed how I viewed my time and my life, I got my drive back. I felt like I was living with purpose again.

Looking toward the future will help you more than looking into the past. Focusing on what you have more than on what you have lost will help you have a vision. Thinking about what could have been prevented many survivors from moving forward. Focusing on how I could get more from the life I had left gave me hope, and it was this hope that inspired me to get up every day.

If you are not going to live your best life for yourself, do it for those who would love to be alive and see you thrive.

Whatever your story, the important part is that you are still alive! The fact that you have made it this far puts you in the category of survivor. Beyond surviving, we must live. Some have experienced way more than others. Some have experienced less, but it was still bad enough to feel like they did not have what it would take to face tomorrow.

I want to talk about the living part after we survive. We need to rejoice because we survived, and we need to fully live the life we were privileged to keep.

Maybe one of these situations resonates with you—or maybe you have a different difficult life story. I am talking about many situations:

- soldiers with posttraumatic stress disorder
- people who are grieving the loss of a loved one
- people who are suffering from depression
- people who were scarred by traumatic childhoods
- people who are grieving a divorce
- people who have suffered a business deal gone wrong
- people who have lost their job

It could be a relationship that ended horribly and left you with emotional scars. The idea of going on a date again seems daunting. Facing the future after loss brings out all sorts of uncomfortable questions and feelings: What if I get hurt again? What if I fail? What if the damage I've suffered can't be repaired? What if I get out there and open my heart up to someone only to end up being ripped apart all over again? What if I start a business and end up losing again? What if it cannot be redone even if I want it to?

I faced fear and challenging questions too. The fear, uncertainty, and anger are real. However, you are alive, and you survived so that you can live.

Irreparable Damages

You might recover from certain losses and move on with life, but you must accept that life never goes back to what it was before. There are things in our lives that cannot be replaced no matter what. Some losses are impossible to recover from. Life will never be the same. With some things in life, once you lose them, there is no way to get them back. You must live with the consequences and do the best you can with what you have. Don't let that stop you from living and finding the good in the life you have remaining.

I often see struggles among women who survived abusive marriages. They do not find joy again when they remarry. I see it in men too, but they tend not to show their emotions.

Some parents struggle to raise their children properly because they lost their own parents when they were young or grew up in a harsh environment. How can you blame them or expect them to model what they never had? It is no fault of their own, because they did not have a role model to follow. I know it is not fair, but it happens.

There are survivors who find love and get married, but they fail to keep their marriage because of what life has taken away from them: the ability to smile without reserve, to place their trust in someone without feeling like they will be betrayed again, to love again, to dream again, or to risk again.

No matter the circumstance, you can commit to living again and finding a new life.

For a long time, I did not think long-term relationships were something of value. I'd lost my father and numerous friends. Even my relationships with my family and friends who survived had changed. Even at their best, I knew relationships couldn't fix the pain I felt.

I would love, and I would date, but I had no plans for long term relationships. However, like anyone else I wasn't going to be here for long and I knew that. But it took some help and some encouragement from family and friends to see that. There is this habit we have when older married couples and sometimes single people who are older than you push you to marry when you are single. I am probably not the only person who finds that habit annoying, but at the same time it can be helpful when you don't see that in your near future. A push can help but what helped me was seeing some happy couples in our church and our community; being the best man for some of my friends; plus, I loved seeing children and I used to spoil my friends' kids and the kids from my family. That helped me believe in long-term commitment.

I eventually found someone I loved and got married. The funny thing is that I have known her since we were teenagers, but we didn't date until our late twenties. I wonder what would've happened if we had dated back then. My fear is that I would've broken her heart, but maybe I would've come back to her—and she would've forgiven me. I am glad that I eventually came to my senses and put a ring on her finger. One of the best decisions of my life.

You may be struggling with moving forward in life, and allowing yourself to love again after a breakup. You may not trust yourself to maintain a long-term relationship because you don't think you deserve it or don't believe you can make it last.

I encourage you to allow yourself to love again and to live again. It doesn't mean you won't be heartbroken or disappointed ever again, but the possibility of joy outweighs the suffering. It can be a fearful thing to allow yourself to open your heart again after multiple disappointments in relationships, but I want to tell you that it is worth it. Healing won't come if you keep hiding, but allowing yourself to love again and to be loved will bring healing to you. Relationships can be like the beauty of a rose and how it is guarded inside thorns. You can't let those thorns stop you from enjoying the beauty of a rose.

What Can We Do?

The Power of Testimony

Sharing what I have been through helped me see past what I'd been through and the choices I was making. As I shared the horrible things I had experienced, people would feel sympathetic toward me. Sharing my story was a chance to hear my own story. It's like someone whose house just burned down, going outside to have a good look at what happened from a distinct perspective. Looking at my own life helped me understand my own struggle, and it connected me to other people who have been through their own struggles.

Whenever you hear about someone who's been through a lot worse than you but has found a way to move on and make something of their lives, it motivates you to make something of your life as well. Some were friends, and others were family members. Some were teachers, and others were preachers. Some were counselors. Their stories challenged me and changed me. Their stories helped me live.

The Power of Information

As a psychology student, I was privileged to have access to information that spoke to my personal issues from an academic perspective.

If you find yourself stuck in the past and can't find the courage to press past those issues, find a trusted circle of friends to share with. Professional counseling is another strategy for healing. You can read books or watch self-help videos on subjects that are relevant to your story and the life you want to live. Understanding oneself builds confidence to overcome life's obstacles and to succeed.

It is vital for a person who has been through trauma to seek medical and professional assistance, including counseling. Some behaviors can be diagnosed professionally. A common diagnosis is posttraumatic stress disorder (PTSD). This can be the result of directly experiencing a traumatic event or witnessing one.

"Post-traumatic stress disorder (PTSD) is a real disorder that develops when a person has experienced or witnessed a scary, shocking, terrifying, or dangerous event. These stressful or traumatic events usually involve a situation where someone's life has been threatened or severe injury has occurred."[1]

Signs and symptoms include losing interest in activities that used be enjoyable, being afraid or suspicious, feeling alone or not wanting to associate with others, suffering persistent pain or headaches, having trouble sleeping, and experiencing memory issues. Other symptoms can be found in the American Psychiatric Association's (APA), *Diagnostic and Statistical Manual of Mental Disorders* (2013).

The path toward healing can include working with a psychotherapist and/or taking medication. Prayer, meditation, worship, or having a trusted prayer partner or minister who is patient enough to listen are all helpful resources. I have found tremendous strength in developing spiritual discipline when it comes to dealing with personal issues, traumatic events, and near-death experiences. These can be less tangible since they work through faith, but healing is healing. When you want your life back, you don't care what hoops you have to jump through to get to where you want to be (provided they fit within ethical and moral boundaries).

The Power of a Good Support System

Overall, know that you are not alone. No matter how painfully lonely you feel today, you are not alone. Life struggles are universal. No person is exempt from them. We are all engaged in the common struggle of living, and you are not alone. I cannot say that enough—and I'm asking you to dare to believe it.

We are going to get through this, and we will make it to the other side. If you do not have anyone who believes in you, let me be

---

[1] https://www.samhsa.gov/mental-health/post-traumatic-stress-disorder#:~:text=Body,or%20severe%20injury%20has%20occurred

the first to declare that I believe in you. I know you are a survivor, and I know there are no strongholds that you cannot break. You are brave and powerful. You are wise and invincible because you are a survivor.

How do I know that? Because you are reading this book—I wrote this book for you. I may not know you personally or know your struggles, but anyone who dares to look to the future has what it takes to succeed. I've seen people succeed, and I've seen people stuck in pain. I've been in both situations. If you cling to hope, know you're not alone, and believe in yourself, you will prevail.

The Power of Faith.

Problems can happen to anyone and they can happen at any time. Those difficult moments in life can sometimes leave us broken, empty, and out of place. It is how we manage such an event that determines how we recover and overcome. That can vary from person to person. It is those who use self-destructive means, such as drugs, alcohol, and other addictive tools to escape the pain that should reconsider their choices and seek professional help.

Being a person of faith in God has helped me tremendously, and I believe it can help you as well. It is when we are struggling with incomprehensible realities that I believe being a person of faith can be beneficial. Without being too technical, I believe that having experienced such a traumatic event as genocide myself, left me with a huge vacuum in my life. A vacuum of fear, uncertainly about life, distrust in humanity, lack of ambition, and so on. I tried to fill that vacuum with alcohol and other things, but the vacuum was never filled. It was only when I became a person of faith that I felt a sense of joy for living and a tremendous peace beyond my understanding. I pray that you find and follow such path as well, and that it will be as helpful for you as it has been for me.

CHAPTER 3

STARTING TO LIVE AGAIN

Life is full of good times and tough times. Mountain moments and valley moments. Painful moments and joyful moments. Moments of sorrow and moments of joy. Some experiences are full of excitement and joy, and others are full of tears and headaches. That is life. The key to overcoming the deep lows is realizing that life is not the ups and downs themselves; life is tough, but you are tougher.

Life is a series of moments and experiences, but it's also a series of decisions. You've been through some dark moments, and maybe you're in one now. You might be stuck, exhausted, or afraid, but there is light and hope. You can find the light by embracing the power to decide and take control of your life.

You get to decide who you are and what kind of future you want. You get to decide and promise yourself that you won't give up. You get to decide to seek help. You get to decide that you will live again.

Get Ready

The daylight is going to come back, and happiness will be part of your life again. Just as the night always comes after the sun goes down, you are certain that the daylight will return in the morning—guaranteed. Do not give up, the daylight *is* coming into your life, and I want you to get ready.

It will not be easy, but it is possible. You can do it. It is going to require your effort and participation—maybe more than you thought possible—but things are going to get better eventually. You need to dig yourself out of any challenging situation life pushes you into.

With God's grace, you will make it.

The goal is clear. It is to live, no more, no less. Here's how to get started.

Step 1: Stop Living in the Past

There is no way we can dwell in the past and change the future or benefit from it. Redeem your time.

Kathryn Sandford said, "Resilient people expect to fail and be disappointed. They know that to be strong, one must overcome the adversity and challenges they face in life. Courageous people choose to 'bounce forward' in life and to keep moving toward living a happy, fulfilled life."[2]

When Nelson Mandela was released from prison, a journalist asked him how he was able to forgive those who had held him in prison wrongfully for thirty years. He replied, "When I was walking out of the door toward the gate that would lead to my freedom, I knew that if I didn't leave behind my bitterness and hatred, I'd still be in prison."

It is admirable how he was able to choose the higher ground to help him move forward, while not allowing the past to steal his present. If he had chosen to hold onto resentment and anger, he would not have been able to become the president of South Africa and an inspiration to many people. He was able to redeem some

---

[2] https://www.lifehack.org/817679/how-to-persevere

of the thirty years he lost in prison by not allowing himself to be a prisoner of the past once he was released from prison.

You can redeem your time by learning how to harness the present. When you focus on the here and now, you have less time to think about the past. When the memories creep into your consciousness—as they are bound to do periodically—acknowledge them for a moment and then bring yourself gently back into the present.

If we crowd our brains, and our lives with hurt feelings, there's little room for anything positive. We can make a choice to continue to feel the hurt or welcome joy back into our life.

Do not allow the past to steal your present and your future. You need to find a way to get rid of any negative energy that pulls you back into the past. It is easy to hold onto anger and resentment, but there is no other way around it; letting go of negative energy, anger, unforgiveness, resentment, and hurt feelings releases some power and strongholds of the offender on you. It helps in releasing the victim from any strongholds that are keeping them down. It allows you to be free to see the beauty of the present time.

Step 2: Cherish What You Have and Not What You've Lost

Try not to focus on what you have lost. Instead, try to focus on what you have remaining. Contrary to some popular advice, do not focus so much on the future that you miss the present.

You need to have a plan for the future, but do not miss the present. Helen Keller said, "Life is short and unpredictable. Eat the dessert first!" She was a political activist and lecturer who was the first deaf and blind person to earn a Bachelor of Arts degree. She understood what it meant to do more with less. Do not allow the worries of what the future holds make you miss the beauty of the present.

Steps 3: Celebrate Every Single Day

Yesterday is gone. Today is at hand. Tomorrow is far, far ahead, and it is difficult for any of us to predict. Today is all you know, and it is all you have. That is cause for celebration—even if today is full of struggle and pain.

> It is essential to understand that we can never live in the past and keep on expecting our future to shine brighter.
>
> —Cherrie L. Moraga

> Happiness is not something you postpone for the future; it is something you design for the present.
>
> —Jim Rohn

> Do not worry about tomorrow, for tomorrow will worry about itself. Each day has enough trouble of its own.
>
> —Matthew 6:34 (NIV)

> Live as if you were to die tomorrow. Learn as if you were to live forever.
>
> —Mahatma Gandhi

There is a reason to celebrate every single day. Think of the many things you have been through that could have claimed your life—you are still here! Deep down in your heart you know that it was not because you were smart or bright, it was by the grace of God that you did not die. That is enough reason to celebrate. Regardless of how life may have been unfair to us, we must celebrate the fact that we are still alive.

Steps 4. Find Your Purpose

Whether you believe in miracles, fate, destiny, or God, you must see that there is value in being alive. There must be a reason you are still alive. Despite what you have endured, you are still here. There must be at least one purpose, and you owe it to yourself and those you love who did not survive to find that purpose and act upon it. You must do as much as you can while you can.

I know you are special. I hope you know that you are special, and even if you do not feel special, I encourage you to find ways to bring your specialness to fruition, and make your survival and all the difficulties you have been through worthwhile. You are a miracle. You probably do not even need me to tell you that because you know it already.

You are still alive for a reason, and that reason is not just so you can eat, drink, and then die. Most people can do that without any effort. Your life cannot be about eating and drinking after all you have been through. You need to recognize that you are special and that you are a miracle.

What will you do with your miracle? What special passion or gift can you bring to the world? How will you live so that others can be encouraged by your story?

You are still breathing, and that is worth celebrating. Think about all the people who didn't make it out alive. Some who were smarter than you, taller than you, or richer than you are not alive, but you are still here. You are reading this book that was written specifically for you. What are the odds?

You didn't do anything special to still be alive that those who passed away couldn't have done. It is just by grace. By grace, we are still alive. You are still alive, and you are still alive for a reason. Now is the time to discover that reason and act upon it.

Commit to finding your purpose and living it.

Step 5: Name the Problem

It's vital to name the pain you're going through, the things you've lost, and the forces that are keeping you stuck. This isn't about blaming your circumstances on others, even when there are people who have harmed you. It's about naming the forces that have taken residence inside you, and are keeping you from having hope, connecting with others, and making positive decisions.

Take some time to think about why you're stuck. It's not about what happened in the past; it's about what's bogging you down now.

From my own experience and those of people I know, I've seen two major barriers to progress.

Barrier 1: No Energy to Fight

We fight hard to survive, and then it is hard to live the life we have been fighting to preserve. Many of us have been through unimaginable things. It may not have been a genocide, but we all deserve to live our best lives without interruption.

Our emotional, mental, and physical limitations can prevent us from reaching our fullest potential. They steal our hope for the future, keep us bound to the past, and prevent us from reaching our dreams and goals. There are too many obstacles, too many struggles, and too many disappointments and headaches. If it is not one thing, it is another.

Barrier 2: There Are No Shortcuts Around Difficulty

There is no easy way through life. You must go through it. It can be mentally, emotionally, and physically draining. If you feel like you don't have the energy to fight, admit it to yourself. Tell people who care about you. Ask for help. Get some rest. Exhaustion is your starting point, but it won't be your ending point.

If you lack energy or feel daunted by the difficulty it would take to recover, don't lose heart. Name the challenge you're facing. Accept the difficulty. Take small steps forward.

As noted earlier, I was privileged to have access to information that spoke to my personal issues from an academic perspective. If you find yourself stuck in what happened to you and can't find the courage to press though those issues, find a trusted circle of friends to share with, and seek professional counseling if possible.

Life sometimes feels like a cup that is so full that a single drop of water would make it spill. In these difficult moments, we cannot afford to give up, especially after all that we have been through. You owe it to yourself to have a life after all you've suffered. If you can't do it for yourself, do it for those you love. Your parents or children might not be here any longer, but they would have loved to see you happy and living your life. Do it for them, if not for you. They would have loved to see you thriving, smiling, winning, and succeeding. They would have been happy to see you going back to school and finish your degree or start a business. They would want you to see you get married and have kids, if possible. Most importantly, do it for yourself, and do it because you can.

Step 6. Steal the Thief

> The thief comes only to steal and kill and destroy.
>
> John 10:10–29 (ESV)

It is still the plan of the enemy of your success to steal from you and see you dead. Since he did not kill you, it is his plan to see you not living. You will not give him that satisfaction, will you? Where can you find the strength to move forward after all your energy has been depleted? Finding the energy to persevere is hard after multiple knockdowns. Les Brown, politician and motivational speaker, said,

"If you fall, fall on your back. Because if you can look up, you can get up."

How do you eat an elephant? One bite at a time. And that's how you are going to beat the enemy to his punch. Life is like a huge mountain that you need to climb, and it is filled with obstacles. After a tragedy, it seems even more like a huge elephant that is standing in your way. Move this mountain like you would eat the whole elephant—piece by piece.

Don't worry about the whole mountain right now. Just look at today. Focus on stopping the thief's next move. Tomorrow, you can face what he brings next. Take it one day at a time.

Step 7. Forgive

After you've done the hard work of digging yourself out from the pain that held you down, after you've begun to live again, one of the most important steps still awaits: forgiveness. Without it, you won't be able to go from surviving to thriving. It's deep and difficult work, but the healing it brings is worth the effort.

> What is forgiveness anyway?
> forgive[3]
> transitive verb
> 1: to cease to feel resentment against (an offender): Pardon forgive one's enemies.
> 2a: to give up resentment of or claim to requital (see REQUITAL sense 1) for forgive an insult.
> b: to grant relief from payment or forgive a debt.

A minister said, "Forgiveness is when you cease to seek revenge for the person who wronged you." That definition hit me with its simplicity and power.

---

[3] https://www.merriam-webster.com/dictionary/forgive

I have always heard that it is particularly important to forgive your offenders and forgive yourself. For a long time, I tried to understand the concept of forgiveness, but it always sounded like putting too much pressure on the victim. If what happened wasn't my fault, why should I be the one who must forgive?

First, how do you forgive those who did you wrong, especially if they never asked you to forgive them or do not care about how they made you feel? They may even be having the time of their life, without remorse or regret. If you finally find the courage to forgive, what if you have no idea of the whereabouts of those who caused you pain? How do you find each other so forgiveness can take place? What if they die before they had a chance to ask you to forgive them, or you to offer that forgiveness to them?

These questions are real, but don't let them stop you from moving forward. Forgiveness is letting go of the hold the past has on you so that you can move forward.

While you are not to blame for what happened to you, you need to find ways to release the pain and hurt the offense has left in you. Forgiveness is not so much about granting pardon to the offender, as it is about setting yourself free from the harmful effects of holding a grudge.

Whether you get to talk to your offender or not, if they are alive or not, it is you who needs to be set free. Forgiving doesn't mean that what happened didn't hurt—and doesn't still hurt—but you're committed to not seeking revenge and not being weighed down by trying to make the other person pay.

Forgiveness is hard, but it's important. No matter what you've suffered, you really can forgive.

Like you, I have been in great pain. At times, it seemed like I could never forgive, but I did, little by little, and I felt freedom, and you can too.

Whether the offender asks for forgiveness or not, forgiving can still be difficult, even when the offender humbles themselves enough to ask for it, which is rare. And if forgiving someone who asks for it can be difficult, imagine forgiving someone who never asks you to forgive them. In some cases, it's hard to know which person to forgive. How could I know all the people who participated in the genocide. That can be hard because some of them died and others fled the country? What does forgiveness look like then?

To make matters worse, sometimes the person who offended you would do it again if given the chance. I was shocked to hear on some social media platform someone from Rwanda saying that if given the chance he would commit genocide again. He unashamedly explained that they understood very well what they did and why they did it—and they would do it again. How do you forgive someone like that?

How do you forgive an abusive friend or partner who never apologizes or keeps doing the same thing? What about a friend who steals from you or refuses to pay you back after you've loaned them money and comes back to ask you for more? Sometimes they may even be angry with you if you refuse to help knowing very well that they failed to pay the first time!

All the above are hurdles of questions and emotion struggles we experience on out journey to forgiveness. And it is a journey. It could days before you come to terms with forgives and it could take years even. Whatever the case may be, don't quit.

I can assure you that it's always possible to forgive, and it's necessary to forgive if you want to thrive.

If the pain they caused is something you are holding onto, you haven't forgiven. You haven't let go.

Part of forgiving is making the choice to switch the way you think about what happened and what you want your future to look like. Refusing to forgive keeps you stuck on the losing side. You need to come to the winning side.

- The winning team doesn't have time to hold grudges because they understand that time is a precious and rare commodity that none of us can afford to waste. Nobody. Holding a

grudge, even for an unfathomable offense, is wasting time and energy that you could use for something better.
- The winning team understands that the longer the offender stays in your thoughts, the more power they hold over you. The winning team dumps the offender out of their mind and body. That's not an easy process, but after the initial moment of forgiveness, whenever thoughts of the offender or offense come up, they recommit to forgiveness and turn their attention to something better.
- The winning team understands that since the offender may have no idea of the pain they have caused, and they may not even care, the winning team works on finding ways to move on.
- The winning team knows that since it is by grace that they are still alive, they forgive because they understood what it is to be given a second chance.

I now understand forgiving those who did not come to ask for forgiveness because I understand that forgiveness is mainly for the benefit of the victim. You need to forgive even if the perpetrators do not ask, because it releases the strongholds the event may have on you. If the person who hurt you is not nearby, hasn't asked for forgiveness, and isn't sorry about what they've done, you can still forgive them. The freedom you'll have as a result is the real purpose of forgiveness—not letting them off the hook for the harm they caused.

It's easy to feel frustrated by a perpetrator who doesn't care about what they've done or isn't asking to be forgiven, but don't waste your time. Staying angry with someone who may not even have a clue or care about your suffering does not make any sense. Why carry that burden all by yourself?

Besides, to people of faith like me, forgiveness is part of the deal. We ought to forgive because we have also been forgiven. That is not hard to grasp. You may struggle with it, but with God's help and the right surroundings, it eventually comes through. This does not mean turning a blind eye. It means you are doing your part to get your life back.

CHAPTER 4

IT IS A NEW DAY!

IT'S A NEW DAY! Now that you've begun to loosen the hold the past has on you, you can begin to live in the present. You can choose to let go, heal, and live. Every day is a new day, and you always have a choice.

Let Go of Anger

Many people say that they have forgiven, but they continue to hold onto that anger. Are you still holding onto your anger? Check yourself every time a situation presents itself that reminds you of the past. When you remember what happened, does the anger surge right back? How about when you meet face-to-face with your offender? Do you feel compassion toward them—or do you feel like you want to take them apart and make them feel the pain they caused you? How do you feel when you meet your ex? The teacher who unfairly failed you? The boss who fired you wrongfully for a job you worked so hard on? The friend who betrayed you when you least expected them to? The family member who keeps causing painful moments in your life?

If you still have a way to go, it's okay. It's important to recognize where you are now, even while committing to forgiveness and letting go of anger. You were hurt badly, and it's okay to feel pain, but the important thing is to make the decision to move forward into health and hope.

I used to struggle with the memory of the genocide and the pain it brought. You can forgive, but how do you get rid of the pain from the memory of your past?

When something tragic happens, most of us harbor painful memories. How do we overcome or manage that painful memory? How do you not feel overwhelmed by sadness or anger? How do you calm the urge to retaliate, especially when you have the means and are in a position to do so? How do you manage the urge to numb your pain through unhealthy means, if they are available to you, since some are harmful and addictive?

Every April, Rwanda holds a memorial for the genocide of the Tutsi. It is an important event because it helps us acknowledge what happened and allows the country to learn from its history. However, it also brings back painful memories for those who lost loved ones. How do we remember without falling back into the pain of the genocide? How do we forgive and not get angry when our memories trigger the pain? How do we forgive and not forget? How do we remember without being angry?

It is not easy to forget. It is unrealistic to think you will forgive and then forget. In many cases, it's important to remember. When Rwandans remember our history, it helps us to ensure that such a tragedy never happens again.

If you forgave the person, it's okay if you still remember the pain. It's okay if you still feel angry or sad at times, and I encourage you to forgive and not forget. Instead, try to release the anger.

After you've forgiven, there are a few keys for releasing the pain, anger, and sadness:

- Decide to stop being a victim and think about who is to blame for your suffering. When you let go of this identity, it opens you up to new identities and new hope for the future.

You're not responsible for what was done to you, but you are responsible for how you respond and what you want your life to be like in the future.
- Focus on the present. You can't forget the past, and it's important to look ahead, but the present moment is the only moment you have. It's the place where you can make a choice about what you think, feel, and do.
- Anger management can help manage the pain of the past.

It may seem impossible to think about what happened without anger or pain, but it can happen when you forgive and commit to letting go of your feelings about the past.

Letting Go of the Past Hurts

The only way to accept joy and happiness in your life is to make space for it. If your heart is filled with pain and hurt, how can you be open to anything new? Make the decision to let it go. Things do not disappear on their own. You need to make the commitment to "let it go." If you do not make this conscious choice, you could end up self-sabotaging any effort to move on from the pain.

In every moment, you have a choice to make—to continue to feel bad about another person's actions or to start feeling good. You need to take responsibility for your own happiness and not put the power into the hands of the other person. Why would you let the person who hurt you have such power over you today?

No amount of rumination has ever fixed a relationship problem. Never. Not in the entirety of the world's history. Why choose to engage in so much thought and devote so much energy to a person who has wronged you?

Focus on the present and be joyful. It is time to let go. Let go of the past and stop reliving it. Stop telling yourself that story where the protagonist—you—is forever the victim of the other person's egregious actions. You cannot undo the past, but you can make today the best day of your life.

Continually Forgive Them—and Yourself

We discussed forgiveness in the last chapter; forgiveness will become a way of life for you. You'll often revisit the decision you made to forgive, recommitting to the choice not to seek revenge. You'll also need to forgive yourself for all the hurt and bruises that come from this journey we call life.

Some of what I write here repeats what I've said before, but forgiveness is so vital that it bears repeating. For many of us, forgiveness is a long process, and that's alright.

We may not forget another person's bad behaviors, but everybody deserves our forgiveness. If we feel stuck in our pain and stubbornness, we cannot imagine forgiveness. Forgiveness is not saying, "I agree with what you did"; instead, it is saying, "I don't agree with what you did, but I forgive you anyway."

Forgiveness is not a sign of weakness. It is simply saying, "You did something that hurt me. I want to move forward in my life and welcome joy back into it. I can't do that fully until I let go of this pain."

Forgiveness is a way of tangibly letting go of something. It is a way of empathizing with another person and trying to see things from their point of view. Maybe they did what they did because of something going on and currently in the life or their past life. It could be due to their upbringing or their surroundings. Poverty, bad politics, bad parenting, mental health issues and more. All those things can cause people to act differently than the norm.

Forgiving yourself is an important part of this step, especially if we blame ourselves for the situation or the hurt we feel. We might have had some part to play in the hurt, but there is no reason to keep beating ourselves up over it. If you cannot forgive yourself, how will you be able to live a future of peace and happiness?

It can be incredibly hard to let go of pain; I have struggled with this myself. If we have held onto it for a long time, it might feel like an old friend. It might feel justified. It might feel sacrilegious to let it go.

Nobody's life should be defined by their pain. It is not healthy, it adds to our stress, it hurts our ability to focus, study, and work, and it affects every relationship we have (even the ones not directly affected by the hurt). Every day that you hold onto the pain is another day everybody around you must live with that decision and feel its consequences. Do everybody else, and yourself, a big favor by letting go of the pain. Do something different today and welcome happiness back into your life.

Help Others Heal

One of the biggest surprises about forgiveness is that it allows you to help others who are struggling. If you're locked up in your own painful past and consumed by anger, you can't help others with their pain. If you forgive, you learn empathy and hope, which can help others.

I am not a doctor or a health advisor who can tell you what to do or how to live your life. No one else is an expert on how to live your life. It is your life, and you know you better than anyone else does. I will share what I did to overcome the scars of genocide. Once you can forgive and let go, the next step is finding a way to help those who also need healing. You can do charity work, advocate for others, or help victims fight injustice; become a source of solutions, not problems. It really helps to see someone else succeeding and knowing that you are part of it. Forgiving what happened to me turned me into a teacher of forgiveness and love.

I was invited to give a talk about love and forgiveness. After the meeting, an attendee asked my host if she could speak with me. The host asked what she needed to speak with me about. The woman said she knew me, and that her family was involved with those who killed some of us and threw us in the septic ditch. I told my host that I did not mind speaking with her because I'd already forgiven them. They showed her into the office, and she fell to her knees and asked me to forgive her and her family for what they had done to us. My presentation had helped her, but she did not want to come out and confess what they had done to me. She felt compelled and pushed to do so, and she did.

I told her that she was brave and that I had forgiven her and her family. How can the forgiven not forgive? She got up, we hugged and cried, and she left.

Because we've forgiven, helping others is a way of life for my wife and me.

My wife, Delice, and I also help new arrivals in our neighborhood navigate the area and integrate and succeed in their new home. These are immigrants who need some pointers and are having a hard time settling in due to language barriers or not knowing how things work. We help with job hunting, college applications, driving, making doctors' appointments, and paying bills.

I am not sure how you are going to help others, but I recommend it. When you experience the freedom of forgiveness, you can have hope and a future. You can help others feel the same way.

Adjust Your Attitude

If you want your future to be different from your past, and nearly everyone does, especially those of us who've suffered greatly, a different outlook on life is needed. Yes, terrible things and unfair things have happened in the past. They have happened to all of us. There is not a single person on earth who can say that they have never cried. The first thing a baby does is cry because life greets them with exposure to things they find uncomfortable. From that time forward, life gets meaner.

We must have a mean and resolute approach to life, with toughness and resilience, while being positive and open. They say, "When life gives you lemons, make lemonade." Life is full of lemons. I think life is a field or a forest of lemons. Bitter lemons leave a good taste once we squeeze them. We can add sugar or water to make it taste less sour.

In other words, with a little work on ourselves, we may be able to make something of our lives despite our past. Once you're on the path to forgiveness, you have a chance for a new perspective.

Beauty doesn't exist on its own; it is created by observers. It is all in the eye of the beholder. You are looking at the event and interpreting it; you can't change what happened or will happen, but you can choose your response. You can choose how you see it.

To be a beholder, you must pay attention. Different beholders might observe events differently. Perspectives make a huge difference in how we live our lives. Everybody has been through something, but the difference is how they perceive it and how they respond to it.

Depending on how you look at it, what you go through may take so much of your energy that it could prevent you from moving forward. We could leave because we survived. At the same time, what happened to us helps us take on life headfirst. The feat, the grace, of having survived gives us the grit and determination to live a full life. No matter what we have been through, how we look at what happened matters.

All of us are affected by our personal experiences in one way or another. How we look at what happened to us is our choice. It may be a hard choice to make, but it is our choice to make. Instead of focusing on the pain of the past, shift your focus to a new beginning.

You have the power to customize how you look at what happened to you. When you put your heart out and fall in love, sometimes it goes wrong, and you end up heartbroken. You could focus on the fact that whoever you were dating broke your heart, made you cry, and might result in you declaring, "I will never allow myself to fall in love again." Or you could say, "Oh great! I am glad that happened, and I still have a life to live. Let me find someone who is worth my time."

After the genocide, I spent so much time trying to make sense of what happened to me and others around me. Were we such bad people who deserved to be killed and wiped off the face of the earth as we were told by the killers? Did God forget about us? Did God decide to give us up to the killers? If that were so, why would God give us up? Did we not pray enough? Were we worse sinners? Surely, we could not be worse sinners than those who did the killing. There is no way.

I blamed God and everyone else for what I lived through during the horrible and unthinkable genocide of the Tutsi. I spent so much time focusing on why it happened instead of focusing on living the life I had left. Consequently, it cost me a lot. Had I known better, I could have maximized my time and focused on what I could do and not on what I was not capable of doing. Instead, I focused more on what I could not do, and I blamed everything else and everyone else for not letting me achieve my goals.

I had enough sense to understand that, but it did not stop me from wondering why it happened to me and why it happened to us. We cannot blame God because he has entrusted the earth to his people. If we try, I think we will turn around and point his fingers back at us.

These kinds of questions have gripped the whole nation, and people have responded in many ways. Some have chosen to forgive and move forward, and some have chosen to cling to anger and pain.

The Rwandans have a proverb: God spends time everywhere else, but he sleeps in Rwanda. After the genocide, someone said that God went around the world to do his errands and forgot to come home—and that is when the genocide started. If that were true, we could stay angry at him and blame everything on him for not coming home to sleep as he had done before.

We sometimes blame the Belgians because they sowed the seeds of division among Rwandans during colonial times. As true as that is, we cannot say that everything is on them. I was not there when they set foot in the country of a thousand hills, but I am pretty sure life was not perfect in Rwanda before colonialism. It was healing for me and for many others when, in 2000, Belgium's Prime Minister Guy Verhofstadt admitted his country's role in the genocide and apologized. Even without that apology, I am responsible for my outlook.

It is good that Belgium and the international community acknowledged their part in this tragedy, but what about us? We had leaders, but it happened anyway. We had churches, and it happened anyway. We had mosques, but it still happened. We had educated people, but that did not prevent it from happening.

How do we know that it won't happen again? Is there any type of assurance we can give to the next generation? What are we doing or not doing to prevent us from going back and repeating the tragedy of thirty years prior? What did we not do that we could've done when the colonials came that could've prevented the seeds of hatred from taking root? What about now? Are we in a position after fifty years to prevent it from happening again? What about all we did on our own despite any outsiders' influence contributing to the problem?

All these questions hinge on our attitude about what happened and how we respond to what we lived through. I cannot make those choices for a whole country, but I can choose how I see my past and how I live my life.

You can choose your attitude, no matter what has happened in your life.

Why you? Why did what happen to you and not to them? Why did they die, and you did not? Why did you survive, and they did not? Why this and not that?

That kind of thinking will get you nowhere, and you need to drop it now. Things happened, and we do not have answers to all the questions. Even if we could find them, you may find that it was not worth your time. Of course, you need to understand what happened and why. It is a normal response to want answers, and it is expected of anyone who experienced something tragic. However, you should not allow it to consume your life to the point that it stops you from living the life you have now.

Change Your Story

It may seem like there's only one story about what happened to you—one simple narrative about what happened, who did it, and how it hurt you—but that's not true. While there certainly are facts about what happened and what didn't, you have the power to customize how you look at what happened to you.

Real healing occurs when we can own up to our mistakes and the realities of our lives, and move on. As helpless as we were and as powerful as the colonials were compared to those they colonized, I still think we helped them in some way. Maybe they sowed the seeds of division, and they probably watered them too, but I am sure we helped the division grow. We should have uprooted that seed of division when we had the chance. Maybe some of us tried, but since I was not there, I do not want to cast blame. We must determine and accept our own contributions to the problem.

In some situations, the victims' actions may not have anything to do with what happened, but that does not stop them from blaming themselves. For those who cannot stop blaming others because of what happened—or for those who cannot stop blaming themselves when they should not—a new way of looking at things is needed for healing to begin.

A new outlook on life is needed if we are ever going to change. Instead of playing the blame game, focus on the present rather than spending time and energy trying to figure out what happened in the past.

It's natural to want to figure out why things went wrong, and it's important to know our history to prevent a reoccurrence of the tragedy. As you are trying to analyze and assess what happened and how it happened, don't get stuck there. You can understand how it happened and make sure it never happens again, but do not allow the past to steal your future. Do not repeat your past mistakes.

What is going to help you move forward is how you look at what happened. Your perspective and attitude determine how what happened matters. We can choose to cry and be unhappy or we can choose to rejoice, because we are still alive and have a chance to make a difference. Rejoice in the fact that we still have time to make our future more joyful, more productive, and more meaningful.

Mourning is part of the healing process, but its purpose is to open us back up to joy. It is possible that the life you have left could be more powerful and more impactful than the one you have lived so far.

What lens do you use? How can you use what happened in the past to fuel your future? It depends on your attitude and how you look at life in general. People do not look at life in the same way, because everyone uses different lenses, angles, and perspectives.

Without the right attitude, we cannot get out. We can keep weeping because we have been thrown into a hole, thinking how life is not fair, or we can embrace the knowledge that it happened, and celebrate that we are still breathing. Guess what? If you still have breath in your lungs, you still have a chance to do something amazing with your life. You are an amazing human being, and you are a miracle.

Life is not fair. What happened to you is not fair, and what happened to other people is not fair. Yet, it did happen, and it does happen, and it will happen. Things happen to people—bad and good.

Let's start finding ways to fight and win. You are a survivor, and you are also a winner. You may not feel like it yet, but you are a winner! Forget those losers who always try to pull you back to how life was in the past. If you ever read the story of the famous son of the carpenter, it is surprising to see how hard it was to be embraced by his own community in spite all the miracles he performed in front of them and for them! Sometime it's those who knew you when back then, who refuse to accept you as the new changed and improved you and can be more and beyond the life they know. If you are careful, they can try to hold you to a lower standard of who you were meant to be. According to the good book we were all created in the image of our Creator. But life experiences, family issues, economic impact, education or lack of it, all play a role in who we are and how much we can achieve in life.

Difficult life experiences can make you think you are not a winner. Life can hand you moments that leave you feeling like you are not a winner. Those moments determine your entire life. You have enough time to recreate your experiences and create winning moments.

That starts today. If not today, when? Tomorrow is not promised to anyone, and all we have is today. Hurry up and start working on your winning moments. Do not worry if it does not come together today, and do not worry if it does not come around tomorrow. Someday, it will come. We must "push until something happens."

How will you push to victory and redeem your time?

CHAPTER 5

FIND YOURSELF AND YOUR VISION

You've survived the unthinkable. You've worked hard to loosen the chains that hold you to the past. It's time to begin to build the life you want.

The struggles we go through change our sense of who we are, and the first step to living the life we want is to recover our sense of self. When we do this, it will lead to a rewarding life.

We can only be rewarded for being who we really are. You will be rewarded for being you, not for being who you are not. You are the best you can be. Nobody can beat you at being you, no matter how hard they try. You are the best you ever created, and there will never be another you.

Dr. Seuss said, "Today you are you, that is truer than true. There is no one alive who is you-er than you."

One of my children was given a prestigious award from her school, the Knox Award, for being kind to everyone, having a positive attitude, and working hard. When we received the email from the teacher, I said, "How amazing it is to be awarded for just being yourself?"

When other people recognize the same qualities in your child and give them an award, it makes you think you are doing something right as a parent. However, even if we have something to do with it as parents, children are their own persons. Parents may contribute to that, teachers may contribute to that, and siblings and friends may contribute to that, but for the most part, it is who they are. It is easy to be who you are.

Our circumstances and our mistakes can lead us to see ourselves negatively. We think it's necessary to change ourselves to be good, but each of us has so much goodness that comes to us naturally. When we nurture that goodness, it grows, and good things come to us.

It is who you are at the core that will be rewarded—not what you want to be.

"Knowing yourself is the beginning of all wisdom," Aristotle said. Knowing ourselves sounds simple, but giving ourselves our attention helps us see the good in us and understand our limitations. When we appreciate ourselves fully, we can manage our time and talents well, which brings joy.

To truly know yourself is the most important skill you can ever possess. When you know who you are, you know what you need to do, instead of looking for permission from others to do what you already know you ought to do. It allows you to bypass frustration, which results from putting time into the wrong things.

Use your reflections to fight your biggest fears. When you understand who you are meant to be, your purpose will become bigger than your fears. When you realize who you are, you will spend less time spinning your wheels. Focusing on your strengths gives you the traction to make a difference in the world. When you know yourself, you will find peace and success.

How to Succeed

Success comes from embracing who we are and not who we pretend to be. Success comes from doing what we are passionate about, which is intertwined with who we really are. A friend used to tell me every time we met that my clothes were me. It always felt good to know that I and what I was wearing were coordinated. In the same way, it feels good when my inner self and my actions match.

We are easily distracted by doing what we are not called to do, what we are not gifted to do, what other people expect us to do, what needs to be done, because we must survive instead of focusing on doing what helps us thrive. Doing what we must do to get by is generally not a bad thing. You do what you must do to be able to do what you need to do and love to do. That becomes a problem when it prevents you from focusing on what you were created to do. The key is to find a way to transition from one to the other.

One of the principal challenges after finding what we are gifted to do and what we are good at and passionate about does not feed us or bring food to the table. You may be the best and most passionate guitar player, but if you don't have anyone to play for, what do you do? That gift may not put food on your table. Do we give up and find a menial job to help make ends meet? How do you transition from living the way you have to, to living to how you were meant to?

- First, would you love to do this even if you were not getting paid?
- Second, there is always a need for your gift on the market, and it is a matter of finding it.
- Third, you may have to package what you have in a way that responds to the market, and not necessarily how you want it packaged if you are not compromising your principles.
- Fourth, maybe someone can help you make the connection between where you are and where you are going or need to be, the jump between the preparation of your gift and your breakthrough. Stay on the lookout.

Who am I? What I am here for?

We're all unique, but in many ways, we have the same purpose. It might take a lifetime to figure out who you are, but you are a great person who has been created to solve problems while enjoying life. That might sound cheesy, but it is true. You were not created to be a miserable person who is here only to suffer and die, even if it feels that way sometimes. You are better than that. You were created to do more.

We have been placed on earth to solve each other's problems. Fathers are solving their own problems and their families' problems. Mothers exist to solve their problems and everyone else's problems. Teachers are here to help us fight ignorance, and bankers are here to help solve our money problems. Politicians are here to help solve society's problems. Preachers are here to help people keep their faith and hope. Police and soldiers are here to protect us.

You fit in somewhere. Your place may be small or large, but it's important. The people in your life need you. The world needs you. You need you. You are one block who is meant to fit in the puzzle called life, so the game can keep going. Your goal is to be busy doing that—trying to find your place in the grand scheme.

Find Out Who You Are

To know who you really are, you must establish who you are not. You are not what happened to you. You are not your experiences. That happened, but that is not you. Who are you? Do you know who you are?

When you ask someone who they are, they might tell you their title, what they do, or what they have accomplished. Who you are is different from what you have accomplished. You are who you are with or without those things. You could be a doctor, but that is not who you really are; that is the title of your profession. You could be a politician, but that is what you do. There is a great person inside of you who has achieved all those things, and that is who you are. That person still exists and has value even if all the titles were taken away from you.

The great person inside of you is who you are. It is not what you do or what people around you think. It is not who society made you, who the circumstances in your life made you, who your family made you, or who your money made you. It is the ideal you, the original person you have been created to be, whether you have a title money or not. It is who you are without those things.

One way to find clues to who we are and what we are good at is to ask the people we trust. If I wanted to find out who you really were, I would ask your parents, spouse, siblings, friends, children, and coworkers certain questions:

- Who do they think you are?
- What do they think you are good at?
- What do they think your strengths are?
- What do they think your weaknesses are?

Compare their responses and look for common characteristics. If four out of five think you are this awesome loving person who can sing and cook, maybe that is who you are. Build your life around those qualities, instead of accepting whatever life throws at you. It is likely that your parents, siblings, spouse, friends, and coworkers know one good thing about you that you have never paid attention to. Try to find what it is and develop it. There could be untapped greatness within you that needs cultivating. Go for it.

Their perspectives are limited, and if what they say doesn't ring true, go with your gut. Being who you are doesn't mean being who other people think you are. Their ideas can help spark understanding, but they can't answer all your questions. Your sense of self must come from inside you.

What Do You Want Out of Life?

Your true self remains underneath all the damage that has been done to you. Begin to look inside yourself. Start with what you do not want. You do not want to die without finding the reason you were born. There is nothing worse than dying before you have lived.

Mike Murdock, an American singer-songwriter and preacher, once said that we are remembered by the problems we have solved or the problems we have caused.

- What problems can you solve?
- You do not want to be remembered by the problems you have caused. You want to be remembered by the solutions you created.
- You do not want to be remembered by the lives you have ruined. You want to be remembered by the lives you have touched and changed in a positive way.
- You do not want your folks to be glad you are gone. Make sure they feel privileged to know you.
- You do not want the person who gives your eulogy to struggle to find out what your life was about. Think hard and project what you want said about you on the day of your funeral.

If your life ended tomorrow, what would your legacy be? If what you see is not what you want, then start working on making it what you want it to be.

What do you want out of life? Why hasn't that happened yet? Those are questions to think long and hard about.

The sooner you can identify what you have been enabled to solve for others, the sooner you will achieve what you want to achieve for yourself.

John Maxwell, a leadership guru, said that you must help people get what they want so they can help you get what you want in life. It is what we were created to do for others that leads us to what we want out of life. All babies are selfish, and that is all right. The problem is when babies become adults and stay selfish. Helping others so you can get what you want is selfish, but that is the kind of selfishness that is good and necessary.

When you have been through difficulties, you feel like you do not have anything to give to others. If anything, you are proud that you can make it from day to day. When you start helping others achieve their goals, life will start happening for you as well.

Dare to Dream Again

After enduring losses, agonies, and struggles, your brain switches to survival mode. You stop loving because you are afraid you will be hurt again. Your brain remembers what happened the last time you tried to love. After so much disappointment, you stop trusting and begin to doubt anyone who tries to connect with you or help, because you know how much trusting cost you the last time. Your brain stops you from taking the chance on love again.

How do we change that? The first step is to acknowledge this pattern and realize that just because something happened once, it doesn't mean it will happen again.

It is hard to dream when life's experiences have not been on our side for a long time, especially when it involves losing those who are close to us. We cannot shy away from dreaming and striving to achieve our dreams because of the failures of the past. Failure and loss are part of the journey. The good news is that you made it out alive the last time, and it is likely you are going to do so again. So why not try?

If you had all the time and money in the world, what would want to achieve? Would it solve your problems and other people's problems? Many things are beyond what you can achieve as an individual. The dream cannot only be about you because that dream would be too small, and most people achieve those dreams without a big struggle.

If what you want is something that would solve your problems and the problems of others around you, you owe it to yourself and those around you to figure it out and do it before you leave this life. That is why you are here. That is why you survived your enemy's determination to kill you. Your enemy failed.

You must find out why you are still here. Many people did not make it, but you did. The fact that you are still alive is an important indication that you have something you are supposed to do with your life. You have a chance to make a difference, and that depends on where you are and which opportunities are present.

- Jesus Christ came to earth to die for the sins of humankind.
- Martin Luther King Jr. died, but he changed the history of America as we know it.
- Nelson Mandela was imprisoned for more than thirty years, but he ended Apartheid.
- Mahatma Gandhi led a peaceful demonstration that led to India's independence.
- The Wright brothers invented airplanes.
- Mark Zuckerberg created Facebook to solve the human connection problems that everyone craves.
- Bill Gates and Steve Jobs created computers and software that changed the way business is conducted and how people live.
- Toyota makes reliable cars that are still affordable.

Those people revolutionized the world, but the inventions did not end there. The less visible people who worked for them made things happen. Jesus changed history, but his twelve disciples supported him and helped him bring about change. MLK was not alone, and Nelson Mandela was not alone. They all had other people working in the shadows to make things happen. We will never know all their names, but they were important.

We go to restaurants to eat and enjoy the service. Even though we might only know the owner or the chef, we know people are working behind the scenes to make things happen. A farmer grew the crops, the clerk sold it, and the driver drove it to its final destination. Just like these people, you have a powerful purpose.

You fit somewhere. People may never know your name, but that does not matter if you do your part and do it well. While doing your best, you might also get some money and fulfillment along the way. That's what life is all about.

Live Your Vision

Now that you've developed a sense of who you are, it's time to bring it into reality. The first step is writing down a vision for your life. A vision is powerful because it helps you focus and inspires you to make decisions. It gives you confidence in your strengths and humility in your weaknesses.

Be specific and detailed. Without a clear written map of where you are and where you are going, it will be difficult to get there. You will not be able to evaluate whether you are on the right track without clarity. The Bible encourages us to have a clear vision.

- "Where there is no vision, the people perish: but he that keepeth the law, happy is he" (Proverbs 29:18 KJV).
- "Write the vision and make it plain upon tablets, that he may run that readeth it" (Habakkuk 2:2 KJV).

Consider these questions:

- What expected outcome would you desire in your life?
- Is it something that is reasonable and achievable?

- If so, what can you do to get it?
- Does it provide the money you need?
- How much money will it take to achieve it? Consider the money and other resources you need to make your vision a reality.
- What are we going to do to get the money? Who do we need to talk to? Do they have money? Can they point us to a person who has money?

Consider the roadblocks you will face. Healing and forgiveness can affect your vision. Identify your areas of failure, heartbreak, and pain. Think about the healing you've experienced in those areas and the hope you're longing for. Include all these matters into your vision.

Write a detailed vision with specifics about what you want your life to be like. If you are going to achieve your goals, you must write down your vision. You must write it down in detailed fashion. It is easy to remember the things you write down, and it is easy to act upon those things.

It helps to measure your progress when you have a written plan and vision. If you do not write it down, how are you going to know if you are close to achieving your dream? You have to be precise when writing down your dream, your vision, and your plans so that everyone can understand them. Do not limit yourself. Consider an old Rwandan proverb: *nta wiyima umwima ahari,"* which means do not limit yourself or deprive yourself of anything. Especially when there is no reason not to dream big. Most of us place limits on ourselves before anyone denies us from achieving our dreams. Write down your dream and make the sky the limit. Shoot for the moon because even if you lose, you will land among the stars.

You need a detailed vision, and you need to make your vision concise and easily understandable. If a ten-year-old can read your dream and understand it easily, then anyone else who reads it will be able to understand it too. If a ten-year-old gets it, then your bankers will get it, your investors will get it, and your supporters will get it. Once you have a written down your detailed vision, practice explaining it to others.

CHAPTER 6

PLANNING AND PREPARING TO THRIVE

Luck is when opportunity meets preparation.

—Seneca

The people who get on in this world are the people who get up and look for the circumstances they want and if they cannot find them, make them.

—George Bernard Shaw

Dream as if you will live forever. Live as if you will die today.

—James Dean

TRAGEDIES TAKE AWAY THE ABILITY to plan, the power of planning, and the belief that there will be a tomorrow—and that it will be good. Tragedy steals the goals, visions, and beliefs. How can you believe in planning when you do not believe you will make it beyond the present day?

It is not that you do not think there is a chance you will be here ten or twenty years from now; it is just that life has disappointed you and you have lost faith in planning for the future. You think the horrible circumstance that stole your past will happen again. If we fail to plan for the long term, the years creep up on us, and then we wonder where all the years have gone.

We think our children are young and fail to plan for college, but before we know it, they are grown and ready to live their own lives. If we had considered it, we could have saved some money for their college or planned our retirement differently. How can you do that if you can't see yourself twenty or thirty years from now? No one thinks about their children's school fund when they can hardly fund their own bank account.

To break your limitation mechanism, you need to recognize that your brain has put you in survival mode to protect you. Now that the crisis is over, survival mode is not where you need to be. You've worked hard to free yourself from the past and look toward the future. To succeed tomorrow, you need to plan today.

Plan Your Way Out

It is possible to go through life and let the years pass with nothing to show for it. You finish school, go to college, and think that everything is going to be as you have planned. You assume you will get a good job, get married, buy a house, and have kids. That is the dream most people have. If you were among those who were not fortunate enough to go to college, you might have dreamed of working hard and getting a break from your own business or from working for someone else.

Everything is possible, but you must plan for it. Nothing worth having ever comes easy. No one ever achieves the life they dreamed of without having planned for it. Even if you were born into wealth, you have to plan and work to keep what you have inherited and grow it; otherwise, you risk losing it all.

If you know it is going to rain, where is your umbrella? If

you really believe in your vision, you ought to have a plan for accomplishing it.

Imagine looking at the weather forecast and seeing that it is going to rain, but you fail to get an umbrella or a coat. That would show that you did not believe it was going to rain. The rain does not discriminate. You cannot afford to not prepare for what is to come.

The Bible says that the rainmaker makes "his sun to rise on the evil and on the good, and sends rain on the righteous and the unrighteous" (Matthew 5:45 NIV).

> One king of old time named Solomon once said, "I have seen something else under the sun: The race is not to the swift or the battle to the strong, nor does food come to the wise or wealth to the brilliant or favor to the learned; but time and chance happen to them all" (Ecclesiastes 9:11 NIV).

Everyone has the same number of hours in a day, but some manage to get more out of them than others. We all have twenty-four hours—no exceptions—and the only difference is how we spend those hours. Without a plan, we risk wasting every minute by doing things that do not matter.

A plan is like a map. It helps you go in different directions and keeps you focused.

There is no such thing as being lucky. What seems like being lucky is being prepared for an opportunity. Lucky people make themselves ready for opportunities. Luck is when opportunity meets preparation. People sometimes wonder how successful people got there. To soothe our inability to plan and work hard, we dismiss the idea by saying that they were lucky. However, there is no such thing as being lucky. If an opportunity lands in your lap, are you prepared for it? If you are not prepared for it, it is a formula for loss and disaster.

Your gift may make room for you, but your gift can take you

where your lack of discipline, attitude, and ignorance may not keep you.

As you plan, it is important to understand your limitations. It is critical to know what you can and cannot do. No one can do it all. With an accurate assessment of what we are and are not capable of, we can plan and execute effectively.

What about the things we could not achieve even if we wanted to? Certain things are going to be out of our reach. There are things your friends can help with, but there are some things they cannot help with. Some limitations are physical, and others are financial. Some may be time related or biological. Sometimes we cannot have it all—even if we try our best. It could be that you want to have children, but your physical or biological limitations will not allow you to give birth. If that is the case, would adoption be a workable solution? If so, that might be a way of achieving what you always wanted.

Jesus told us to assess our abilities before going into battle:

> "Suppose one of you wants to build a tower. Won't you first sit down and estimate the cost to see if you have enough money to complete it? For if you lay the foundation and are not able to finish it, everyone who sees it will ridicule you, saying, "This person began to build and wasn't able to finish."
>
> Or suppose a king is about to go to war against another king. Won't he first sit down and consider whether he is able with ten thousand men to oppose the one coming against him with twenty thousand? If he is not able, he will send a delegation while the other is still a long way off and will ask for terms of peace (Luke 14:28–32 NIV) back."

Isn't that good advice? If you don't think you have what it takes to fight this battle, ask for peace. You need to know what you are capable of and what you are not capable of and then decide accordingly.

Understand what you have and what you do not have. If you understand your limitations, you know that there is nothing else you can do. That would be a good time to seek resources outside of yourself.

One way to maximize your time is to project the end of your life and plan it from the end to the beginning. What if the next three years were the only years you had left to live? At the end of those three years, you might be given more time if the three years have been maximized. Did you do what you were created to do? Did you always do the right thing? How different would your life be? What would you do differently? Would you love more or forgive faster? Would you make sure your family lived in a safer place after you were gone? Would you visit your parents more or hug and kiss your children more? Whatever your thing is, that is exactly what you need to do.

Not everyone will be gifted three additional years. Some people might only have a day, and others might only have a year. Some will live longer, and some will not. Nobody knows what tomorrow will bring, but we can all agree that we cannot waste today. If we maximize today and tomorrow, people will say we have lived our lives to the fullest. That is what I wish for you.

Connect with Others

One of the best ways to deal with your limitations is to connect with others. Understanding our limitations helps us know when to involve others. Nothing is impossible, because if we are limited, somebody else might be able to step up. If we can connect, we will become unstoppable. You cannot do it all, but you can do something.

It is healthy to ask for help. Pride can get the best of us, and we can refuse to ask for help when we desperately need it. Everybody needs help in some way.

It is especially important to connect to people who are excited about your dreams and projects. Avoid the ones who are jealous and negative. Find people who are willing to go with you anywhere—even if the plans are not in their interest. Many people around us are there because they have received help from us in some way. They only stay with us as long as they benefit.

Try to find two or three people who will stay with you even when things go in a direction they do not desire. If such magnanimous people are around you, consider yourself blessed.

Not everybody will be happy about your dream. Many would love to see you fail, especially if they have tried and failed themselves. Find people who want you to succeed.

The pain of lost connections can make it difficult to achieve our dreams, so be bold enough to connect with others. What about people who lost parents and still feel the emptiness, since a parent can't be replaced? I lost my father during the genocide, and it has affected me negatively in so many ways. I have had many role models to fill that gap, and my life is probably not that much worse than it would have been if he were still alive. Of course, it is not the same, but it is a limitation that became manageable once I learned to recognize those who were sent by God to fulfill that role.

If you look closely, you may find that God sent people to you. They have come to fill the gap of the one you lost. A child can bring joy and help you forget the people you have lost. God might use a husband or a wife or a child or a friend to fill the gap. It will not be the same, but it can help. I pray that God will fill that gap in your life so you will be lacking nothing.

Time for Action

You've found your gift. You've written it down. You've planned and prepared. You've connected with people who can help and support you. The only thing left to do is act.

Work your gift until it becomes you.

Once you find what you are good at, spend time investing in what you like to do. Whether you get paid or not, the important part is that you are doing what you were created to do.

Planning requires faith, but faith without action is irrelevant. The Bible says it is dead. Mother Teresa responded to a need. She did not get paid, but she wasn't broke either. Once you step into what you were called to do, money becomes less of an issue. There is plenty of money in the world, but we must find purpose for it.

Once you figure out what you are supposed to do, have a vision and a plan for how to get there. The next step is acting. Nothing just happens. We see the product of people's work. Somebody must do it; otherwise, it would not get done. You must act. No one achieves anything by being in a perpetual state of dreaming.

> Faith without works is dead. What good does it do, my brothers, if someone claims to have faith but does not prove it with actions? This kind of faith cannot save him, can it? Suppose a brother or sister does not have any clothes or daily food and one of you tells them, "Go in peace! Stay warm and eat heartily." If you do not provide for their bodily needs, what good does it do? In the same way, faith by itself, if it does not prove itself with actions, is dead. (James 2:14–17 ISV).

Use short-term and long-term planning to achieve your goals. Planning when you have been through a lot is not easy. Whatever you went through might have taken away your ability to trust and imagine a future.

You need to write a vision for your life, plan for it, gather others around you, and act on it. A miracle is inside you, and even the hardship you've been through can't destroy it. You are going to need people to help you put the plan into action; you cannot do it alone. You need to connect with the people who will connect with the people who will help you get there.

One Point in Time

I was a janitor while I was in college to help pay the bills and buy gas. I asked my boss to give me a raise because he was giving me more work than usual. He told me that he was not going to give me a raise and declared that I did not need one. He said that I had so much potential, and I was wasting my time trying to get a raise out of him. He said that I looked like I could do better with my life than being a janitor. That shocked me because he was my boss. I assumed his advice contrasted with his interests. He was honest and truthful, and he would not have said it if it were not to his advantage.

I quit my job the next day. I was confused but inspired by the idea of having the potential to succeed. I went home and sat down in my room in complete silence with the lights out to help me think and reflect. The next day, I started applying for jobs that I thought would give me exposure to other opportunities, especially ones that involved more interaction with people. I wanted to perfect my English, which I believed was a necessity for my success.

I got a job at a car rental company at the airport. My English was not bad, but my computer skills were horrible. I lost that job after three weeks because it was too much for me. My charming and charismatic personality got me the job, but my poor computer skills got me fired. I left that post and moved on. It was kind of a difficult job, and I was not prepared, and their training was close to none. Learning the computer program in advance might have taken about a week, but I hadn't thought about it. I just wanted a job, and I got it. They could have prepared me better, but I still see that as my own responsibility.

I got a job selling furniture, and the company used a similar program. I kept that one because I had improved, but I still needed training in other areas. My manager noticed that my computer skills and my English were good, but my personality was going to be an issue. I asked them to give me more time to perfect my skills. I was a quiet type, and there was no way I was going to be able to convince buyers if I was not more outgoing. They used to make me stand at the back of the building, and the manager would stand at the front of the building and make me shout my lungs out. They realized that I was good at selling, but I was a bit shy. I was good at it because what I had done before was harder. I had sold things door-to-door, and selling furniture in a store was simple. I was gifted at selling, but I needed to work on my voice.

Through these experiences, I learned to write a vision, prepare, connect, and ask for help. They were the foundation for all the successes I've had since. I've repeated the process many times, and you too can make your vision a reality. You might have to train yourself to overcome any limitations if you are going to maximize the time you have left on earth.

CHAPTER 7

MANAGE, INVEST, AND ENJOY

Once you're living your vision, you still have more to do. You need to maintain it, invest in it to make it grow, and enjoy it, because that's the whole point of thriving after all you've lived through.

You need to know what you have. Resources are limited. Nobody has complete control. Think about what you have, and don't get stuck on what you don't have. All of us have the same amount of time, and it is a limited resource for everyone. Our health has a limited time span and will run out eventually. There is never enough money, but if it is managed well, it can last and be used effectively. People can make you or break you. They are the most valuable resource in life. The key to success is managing what you have, finding what you need, and not getting hung up on what you don't have.

Build Positive Relationships

We all need people in our lives. You cannot make it in life by yourself. Even when you've been hurt and survived so much on your own, people are the key to your success.

Life brings people into our lives, and they are a gift. They need to be taken care of and managed well. Parents and siblings are a gift. Teachers and students are a gift. Friends and coworkers are gifts. In life, we meet bad people and good people. They all need to be managed. The help we need to achieve the next step often comes from the people we least expect to help us. You can never tell who God will use to help you get to the next level in your life.

Making the most of the people in your life requires forgiveness and compromise. It requires conflict resolution, effective communication, and negotiation. And trust.

As you try to achieve your dream, you will encounter obstacles, and some of them will be created by the people around you. There will always be some people who will try to sabotage your plans. Watch out for those with different agendas who are trying to attach themselves to your business to enhance only themselves.

Learn to trust others—and learn to trust your own judgment and your vision for your future.

Grow Your Skills

Sustainability is how you stay afloat. Despite the skills you have now, you're going to need training. Without continual training, there is no way you can compete in the marketplace and be sustainable for the long haul. The world changes every day, technology changes every day, and there are multiple discoveries every day. To sustain your success, you have to build on it. You are going to need training to compete in today's market.

When most businesses started selling online, Sears was reluctant to join the online market; therefore, they found themselves behind and ended up closing their stores even though they were one of the big retailers in the United States for decades.

Take a class, go to a seminar, listen to podcasts, research online, or watch videos. Many videos can train you in different things, providing you a way to sustain your achievements. You must be educated to stay on the cutting edge of technology. I always joke that I can cook anything, as long as I can watch a YouTube tutorial first.

During the COVID-19 lockdowns, many businesses had to close. The companies that were working online actually benefited. Companies like Amazon increased their revenue, but those that were limited to physical locations ended up closing. If you are not prepared or trained, you are going to be left behind—and everything you worked for could be lost. We are online all the time anyway. Why not use some of that online presence to better yourself? Check out podcasts, see how what you do is done in other places, attend seminars, read books, and find mentors. Otherwise, you might be left behind.

Assess your current skill level and how it matches your long-term goals. What do you need to learn to get where you want to go? Make a plan and stick to it. Friends can hold you accountable for your plans.

Perseverance

Persevering through hard times requires a "never give up" mentality. There will always be problems and challenges, and we will always have to figure out a way to resolve them. The problems might be with the people we work with or live with. Some problems might relate to our health, emotions, or finances. Managing the problems that come our way gives us the green light to keep moving ahead.

When we've been through trying times, we might feel too tired to endure more difficulties. We might think we have a right to an easier life. That's just not the case. As you heal from what you've been through, your resilience will grow. As you accept that difficulty is inevitable, you'll be able to rise to the challenge.

My kids always try to get me to play video games with them. The mission of the games is to persevere. To keep playing, you have to keep your agent from being killed by your opponent. You have to keep dodging things he throws at you, go over mountains, and overcome obstacles. The more challenges you overcome, the farther you get to go in the game.

I think the designers of the game are modeling life in general. The things we overcome give us the energy to keep moving forward. A lot of that depends on how well we know ourselves.

What do you do when you are depressed or sad? Do you have a strategy to shake off the feeling or do you crawl away and hide? Do you have a plan for the inevitable or take life as it comes? I encourage you to come up with a plan for every trouble you might encounter.

Reevaluate

You also need to periodically reevaluate your plans. Take some time to look back and honestly evaluate what you've achieved so far. Ask yourself if you are any closer to achieving your goals. Look at the past year and try to evaluate yourself.

- Are you where you are supposed to be?
- Are you going in the right direction?
- Is there anything that needs to change?
- Are there things you need to stop doing because they are not helping you achieve your goal?
- Are there things you need to focus on?

You need to take time to do an honest evaluation. You may need to ask other people or create a survey to elicit honest opinions.

You cannot maximize the time you have left on earth if you do not evaluate and make the necessary changes. You could be letting time slip through your fingers without knowing it.

We can get distracted by doing good things that have nothing to do with our destination or that are not in line with our goals and plans. Since you do not have that much time to work with, plan for it, and make sure you are spending it wisely.

We don't realize how short life is until it is too late. Young people have a different sense of urgency because they don't understand how short life is. When we are young, we want to have fun, because we think there will be enough time to be serious later. Only as people age do they focus on not wasting time. Young people think they will always have enough time, only to wake up with no time.

How much would you accomplish in a day if you lived each day as your last? With all you've survived, you know that life is fragile and fleeting. Use that knowledge to your benefit as you pursue your goals.

Invest Your Resources

Investing in yourself will increase your value. The most important investment we can make is in ourselves. The more valuable you are to others, the more profitable you will be.

Everyone has twenty-four hours, but the value is different for each of us. A lawyer can charge you $500 an hour, and you will pay it because you've decided that their help is that valuable to you. A business consultant can charge you thousands of dollars, and you will pay it because they have the knowledge you need to get your business to the next level. Different actors can perform in the same movie but get paid different rates, depending on how valuable they are perceived to be.

You can increase your value by increasing your self-value. A chef can increase their value by learning to cook better or learning more skills. A doctor may increase their value by specializing in a specific field. If you are a bus driver, you might find better job options if you took a driving safety course. If you sell food in an open market, you may increase your value by learning how to better package what you sell.

Whatever field you are in, there are steps you can take to become more valuable to the people you are called to serve. You can always increase your options by increasing your knowledge. It may require connecting with a mentor or enrolling in a course.

We have more options today than anyone who came before us. Online learning offers all kinds of videos about various subjects. Numerous people create content and share their knowledge to help others and themselves. Not everything you find online is going to be beneficial and correct, but with due diligence, you can find helpful information, sometimes for free.

Invest Financially

Learning about financial investing is important for maximizing your time. The strength you have today will diminish, and the beauty you have will vanish, but if you have sound financial investments, they will grow stronger if they are managed well. You can only achieve so much with the knowledge, strength, and energy you have. With investments, you can multiply the return exponentially. Your investments can even outlive you if you invest properly. If you have children or are planning to have children, you should be thinking about how you are going to take care of yourself, your children, and your grandchildren. That can only happen if you invest, and if your investments outlive you. "A good man leaves an inheritance to his children's children: and the wealth of the sinner is laid up for the just" (Proverbs 13:22 KJV).

You can take advantage of multiple venues for investments. Whatever you choose, make sure it is something you understand. Understanding your investments is going to require training. With the right information, you can make the right decision. You will also need to connect with people who are knowledgeable about investing, whether it be the stock market, real estate, bitcoins, or something else. You might have to hire them, but you also must learn it yourself, or at least make sure it makes sense to you.

What should you invest in? Real estate is one of the simplest investments you can start with, since we all must live somewhere. By buying a piece of property, you guarantee yourself a place to live while growing your investment. If you work hard and make it pay off, your children may not have to start from scratch like you did. If you become comfortable and knowledgeable in the subject, you could even try to buy more than one property and grow your portfolio. Education and connecting with the right people are important.

Other options are stocks, mutual funds, bonds, gold, and cryptocurrency. Whatever direction you decide to go, make sure you understand it before you invest. Make sure you're investing, so your money can work for you, instead of you working for your money for the rest of your life. Time is a limited resource that must be managed with caution and wisdom.

Take Care of Your Body

You only have one body, and that is it. Taking very good care of that body may be the best and easiest investment to make. You must take care of yourself. You need to eat right, exercise if you can, get adequate rest, take showers, dress nicely, brush your teeth, get a yearly checkup, and spend time outside.

What if you work hard, become a millionaire, and die young? If your body is not healthy, you are not going to be able to achieve anything. You must be healthy to enjoy the fruits of your labor. Otherwise, everything is meaningless.

One aspect of health that many people overlook is rest. Knowing when to stop is important. You must stop and get some rest to replenish yourself. Rest helps you reenergize yourself. Without rest, everything you are trying to achieve will amount to nothing.

There are so many threats to our bodies. The food we eat might not be processed right. There are accidents everywhere. Even if we take care of ourselves, sickness can come from out of nowhere. It is our duty to take care of our bodies as much as we can.

Without your body, there is nothing else that can be done. The greatest investment in every human being is their body. When you have your body, you can breathe and do a lot of other things. If you do not have a healthy body, you will be limited in what you can achieve. Life is the first and most expensive investment afforded to everyone. Therefore, it is worth cherishing as much as we can. May you be granted good health for the rest of your life.

Feed Your Mind and Spirit

You need to feed yourself spiritually, take care of your body physically, and guard your mental capacity. You need a sharp mind to face life. Life is tough, and it takes a tough mind to tackle it. If you are not mentally capable of doing things, there is not much you can do. That is why you need to educate yourself as much as you can. The world changes by the second, and we have no choice but to change with it. You need to train your mind in practical skills, nourish your mind, and make time for fun and rest.

Own things, but do not let them own you. No matter how much success you have, no matter how much money you have, and no matter how many things you have, there are things that money cannot give you. If you cannot get something physically, you might try to get it spiritually. You need both.

You need to find a source of happiness that lasts a long time, regardless of what you have. It is dangerous and unwise to base your happiness on material things that are temporary. What will happen when those things change, get lost or lose value? Are you going to lose your peace as well? I am not trying to scare you and say that you will someday lose it all, but it happens.

After surviving so much, your inner spirit can feel overwhelmed or detached. Feed yourself spiritually so that you can fully engage in life.

Different people have different ways of feeding themselves spiritually. Spirituality differs from person to person. Spiritual food brings you what money, sex, and power cannot buy. There is a sense of peace that can only be gained spiritually. Peace is not centered on material stuff, achievements, family, politics, social status, or school degrees. Peace lasts even if you lose everything. You might not have any money, or your closest friends and family have passed on, but there is a way to sustain peace from within. Find the peace that passes all understanding (Philippians 4:7 NIV).

How do we find this peace? Long-lasting happiness lies within, and it comes from knowing and accepting who you have been created to be, doing what you have been created to do, and recognizing and acknowledging your Creator.

Not everyone believes in the same things. Some believe, and some do not. Some believe that God exists, but others do not believe there is a Creator above all of us, and that is the way it is for them.

Whatever you believe in, and however you believe it, we all need a way to help us back to the center of our souls when things go left or right. Trying to control everything would be harder if you did not believe in a power above you.

Whatever you do to help you center yourself, I encourage it. Some people turn to music, as it helps them feel centered. When everything around them crumbles, music calms their nerves, which is good, especially if they play an instrument. Others play sports or create art. Whatever helps you feel centered—and is not self-destructive—I support. You need that. We all need a way to find peace amid life's chaos.

From my perspective, I believe that having faith in Jesus gives us the power to become more than what we are. That has actually helped me and molded me into who I am today. The wisdom of his teachings, his standard of discipline, his ability to focus, his demand to choose a higher ground when confronted with difficult choices or conflicts with people, his service to humanity, and his grace are invaluable. The guidance and empowerment of the Holy Spirit are afforded to all those who believe in the Son of God. I highly recommend embracing them and seeing how far they can take you.

I am not recommending that you become a religious person, but rather a person of faith that is active, because faith with no action becomes meaningless. Faith with a prayer life, led by the Spirit of God and backed up with action is what I am talking about. "This beneficial relationship, sometimes referred to as spiritual support or positive religious coping, has been found to be generally related to better functioning after trauma, including posttraumatic growth. This may happen as people increase their faith as it becomes even more meaningful to them, finding a great sense of purpose in life, closeness to a Higher Power, and sense of collaborating with a Higher Power to solve problems."[4]

Invest in Others

How do we help others find peace and stay grateful? How are you going to help more people like you get out and stay out? "It is more blessed to give than to receive" (Acts 20:35 NIV). Remember to give back. You want to give back, and you need to give back. If you do not give back, you will only be cheating yourself. There is a level of fulfillment in giving back that you cannot find anywhere else.

Even bad people who do terrible things to earn a living find fulfillment in giving, because it feeds their good side and makes them look good. A good person who gives back gets a double reward. You must give back because you get more when you give back; the joy you receive can never be duplicated.

A successful businessperson might help someone else succeed. Seeing that person succeed will give them a sense of happiness that cannot be taken away. That will motivate them to do even more and

---

[4] https://www.ptsd.va.gov/professional/treat/txessentials/spirituality_trauma. asp#:~:text=Spirituality%20can%20be%20helpful%20when,comfort%20 during%20times%20of%20distress

will increase their sense of purpose. After all, we were all created to help each other in one way or another.

Enjoy Your Life

Make fun a priority. Whatever you are doing, planning to do, or will do, if you are not having fun doing it, then it is not worth it. There is no point in doing anything if it is not fun.

If you do not design your life around what makes you happy, how do you expect it to happen or be sustained? Life is about every man for himself, and no one out there wakes up with a focus on your happiness except you. Therefore, plan to be happy, and design your life to be that way.

A wise person said that life is so short that we cannot afford to live it unhappily. What is the point if you are to achieve all there is to achieve in life only to end up being miserable? If what you're doing is not enjoyable, you need to make a change. I believe you would rather have little money with peace than have riches with no peace.

> Better a dry crust with peace and quiet than a house full of feasting, with strife (Proverbs 17:1 NIV).

How do you spell fun? Life is serious business, but without fun, it cannot be a success. Material success, financial success, power, and influence cannot purchase a small piece of happiness. Some people seem to possess everything in the world, but they end up killing themselves because they do not have peace and joy within.

Real peace is the kind of peace that you cannot put a price tag on, and it cannot be taken away, even if you lose all that you have achieved. Real peace only comes from being in sync with who you really are and doing what you were placed here on earth to do. You will never find a fish that is sad when it is in the water, because that is where it was designed to live. An eagle would be miserable if you were to take its wings and force it to walk on earth like a chicken.

What can we do to find priceless peace and joy?

- Refuse to be who you were not meant to be for even one more day.
- Allow your heart to believe and be guided by the voice of your Creator, which lives within you and has been calling you to greatness.
- Find out what you have been created to do—and do it. Life is so serious. If you are not having fun, then there is no fun in living it.

This may be 360-degrees turnaround for some people, but the decision to focus on achieving peace will definitely be worth it. It could mean changing friends or leaving the friends who do not enjoy the real you, and only want to hang out with you when it is convenient for them.

If you are not having fun doing something, what is the point of doing it? If what you are doing does not bring a sense of fulfillment to your life, you are not having fun. You need to stop doing that and find what brings you fulfillment. Life is too short to spend it unhappily, and living without any enjoyment is not worth it.

Many people do lots of things for riches, glory, and power. However, once they achieve that, they are unable to enjoy themselves because fun was not part of their plan.

You may have to reinvent your journey if the one you're traveling on is not enjoyable. You may have to find ways to make it enjoyable. There are always ways to enjoy what you do. If not, maybe it is time to make the necessary changes and find a way to live that speaks to who you are. Do the things that bring fulfillment.

Most of the time, we do not do what lines up with who we are because we want to maintain the status quo. Being the president of a company may be miserable for you, but you cannot allow yourself to step down and work in a different role that is less stressful because of the pay level and the lifestyle you have built around it. Is that worth being miserable?

A lower-level job may not be fulfilling for you. Do you aspire to lead, but you feel stuck in a lower-level job? Why not work hard so that you will become more valuable to the marketplace. What if they cannot afford to *not* promote you? For some people, being a leader may be fulfilling, but for others, being a lower-level worker may be more peaceful and less stressful. A supporting role would be the best position for some people, but a leading role might be the best for others.

Some teachings encourage people to work for themselves and be entrepreneurs as a path to happiness, success, and fulfillment. This may be true for some, but it cannot be true for all. Being a business owner is not as fun as you think. Being your own boss with no one to tell you when to go to work and so forth may sound tempting, but you should talk to those who are doing it before you envy them. I have been my own boss, and I have had jobs where I had to respond to someone else. Find what fits you best.

Some people should not work for other people because they're better suited to working for themselves. They say that entrepreneurs are usually bad employees, and good employees are bad entrepreneurs. I do not know if that is set in stone, but whatever you do, make sure it lines up with who you are. If it doesn't, you need to make changes. At the end of the day, you want to live a life you love and love the life you live.

Embrace Obstacles

Obstacles are part of the fun. Playgrounds are designed for kids to have fun. They have lots of obstacles, mountains to climb, and caves to hide in. Adults are the only ones who see obstacles in life and start to groan. Children thrive when faced with obstacles. Life is a huge playground that is filled with obstacles and hidden curves and caves. I think life was created with problems so that we would have fun solving them. Many adults lose the child-like type spirit and innocence and lack of fear and luck of shame within them at an early age, then revert into a life full of fear, doubt in their own ability, not sense of dreaming for the impossible which ultimately lead to a life full of much disappointments, sorrow and painful experiences. We need to bring a children like spirit back into our lives.

Kids have fun all the time. No matter how poor a child is, if their basic needs are met, and there is no abuse, they are typically happy. They see a mud puddle, and all that goes on in their mind is fun, but all that goes on in the adult's mind is dirt. They think fun, and we think dirt. They see a tree and think of climbing, and we think of falling; they see a cave and think of playing hide-and-seek, and we think of being lost.

We run to lose weight, and it feels painful, but they just run all the time for the sake of running. They run, fall, and get bruised, and they are back at it as soon as someone puts a bandage on the wound. They forget it even happened. When adults get a wound, they hold onto that pain forever. It prevents them from daring to enjoy themselves again.

Be a kid again and again and again. No wonder the good book says we ought to have the faith of little children as a prerequisite to being part of the kingdom of winners.

CONCLUSION

You can win against all odds if you defeat the victim mentality.

Life can be brutal, harsh, and unfair. What did we do to deserve what happened to us? What did you do to deserve whatever happened to you? Most likely nothing. You're not perfect, but you are not the worst person in the world. We are all here by grace.

Those who seem the worst in our eyes seem to be getting away with so much, while the good ones are stuck, but the rain falls on the just and the unjust (Matthew 5:45 NIV). Life isn't fair. It will knock you down when you least expect it, and leave you lying in the gutter to fend for yourself. You can choose to be a victim of circumstance or get up and keep going. It's that simple.

We can't afford to live a life that is full of excuses. It is easy to join the people who play the victim, and if you look closely, you will see that they make a lot of excuses. Without accepting responsibility and taking matters into our own hands, we won't go anywhere. Those who know that life is a gift, no matter how it looks, will thrive against all odds.

There is a purpose to your life, and it is worth finding. Finding your life purpose may seem like a tall order, but it's already within you. Trust that you're on the right path. Think about what makes you happiest in life—the things that tug at your heart and make you feel. As Thoreau said, "Go confidently in the direction of your dreams."

Build a Positive Mindset

1. Don't waste time. Time is your most valuable asset. Don't waste it. One of the biggest regrets people have when all is said and done is how they spent their time. If you want to live without regrets, start asking yourself one simple question often: "Is this the best use of my time?"
2. Step out of your comfort zone. To live without regrets, you need to be bold and take risks. No one achieves greatness by sitting back and playing it safe.
3. Cut the fat. This may be a tough pill to swallow, but there are people in your life who are holding you back. Choose to spend most of your time with positive people. Negative folks will only bring you down.
4. Visualize. What you think becomes your reality. Creative visualization is one of the most effective techniques for harnessing the power of your mind. You possess an amazing gift: the ability to create by using your brain. Use it.
5. Make time for family and friends. Relationships are one of the keys to happiness. In *The Top Five Regrets of the Dying: A Life Transformed by the Dearly Departing*, one of people's top regrets was not staying in touch with friends. To live a life without regrets, spend more time with people you love. "(https://bronnieware.com/blog/regrets-of-the-dying/)"
6. Live in the present. Eleanor Roosevelt said, "Yesterday is history, tomorrow's a mystery, and today is a gift, that's why it's called the present." Enough said.
7. Ask questions. Assumptions are the most dangerous thing in the world. Don't assume. Ask.
8. Do what you love. I talk to people all the time who are "stuck" in jobs they hate. If this is you, do something about it. Start a side gig by working on a project you're passionate about.

9. Take care of yourself. Your health is a gift. Do yourself a favor and start eating real food instead of processed, fake junk. And get up and move. Sitting too much can literally kill you.
10. Never stop learning. One of the secrets to living a life without regrets is to learn as much as you can about everything you can. You'll find wisdom in the most unlikely places if you're willing to look.
11. Go out of your way to help others. Helping other people get what they want is the key to getting what you want. The world doesn't revolve around you or me. Make the world a better place for others, and the universe will reward you.
12. Focus on the little things. One of my favorite quotes is from Henry Wadsworth Longfellow: "The heights by great men reached and kept were not attained by sudden flight, but they, while their companions slept, were toiling upward in the night." Take small steps every day toward achieving your goals. These "little things" will compound into monumental achievements if you keep repeating them.
13. Believe that the path you're on is the right one. At the end of *The Count of Monte Cristo*, Edmund Dantes (The Count) says one of the most memorable lines in literary history: "All human wisdom is contained in these two words: 'wait' and 'hope.'" If you think and hope you're meant for something bigger.

APPENDIX

My Testimony: I Barely Survived

People ask me how I survived the genocide against the Tutsi in 1994, but I do not know if the right way of putting is that I survived or that I was buried and just happened not to die. Yes, I survived, but I was surprised that I did. I thought I was never going to see the light of day again, but somehow—by the grace of God—I lived. I am glad I can tell you my story.

My story is not that different from most people who survived the genocide against the Tutsi. All the stories are painfully and infuriatingly sad. Whenever a survivor tells their story, no matter who they are or when I hear it, I always cry. I feel sad and angry, but I am glad to see that they survived to tell their story.

In the Ring of Fire

On the morning of April 7, 1994, around five or six in the morning, my father woke us up and told us to get dressed. We asked why, and he said that the president's airplane had been shot down by people who were not known. Right there and right then, I knew the moment we had been waiting for was here. The war had been wearing on, and we knew a breaking point would come that would put our family in grave danger.

As everyone was scrambling to figure out what to do, afraid of what was about to happen, my father divided us and had us go our separate ways. My dad said, "Even if some die, some may survive."

My four siblings and I tried to go different ways and we hid in the bushes for a while. We desperately looked for places to hide, and we eventually found ourselves in a neighbor's house. She was one of few who did not believe in killing due to her Christian faith, even though her siblings were involved. The people who were doing the killing were a group called the Interahamwe, a militia that was supported by the government.

The Interahamwe militia found our father and killed him, and then they came for us at our neighbor's house, where we'd been hiding for almost a month. We did not get to mourn our father's death or bury him. We got news of his death from the woman who was hosting us, news that she'd heard from people at a roadblock.

We didn't have the luxury of crying or mourning his passing. The only thought in our minds was that they would be coming for us next. They made his death sound like it was a relief. Basically, since they had already killed him, we shouldn't worry too much. We knew that our days were also numbered. There was no room to mourn; all we could do was wait for our time to come.

Eventually, the government soldiers who were camping nearby received a tip from one of our neighbors that we were still alive. They were also told that one of our family members was part of the army they were fighting, and he might be coming to rescue us. They came for us—my second big brother, my sister, our youngest sibling, and our pregnant mom, and me—as quickly as possible.

The soldiers banged on the door and told our host that they were looking for some government accomplices she was hiding in her house. One of the soldiers added that they knew our brother was part of the rebel army and had been shooting at them. Since they had lost their positions, we had to pay for their losses.

At that point, there wasn't much she could do but comply. If not, she would be killed along with us. All of us came out from hiding, and they made us form a single line. They told us to go in front and kept pushing us with the handles of their guns. They led us to a refugee camp that was about a fifteen-minute walk. It took us about thirty minutes since we were walking and being interrogated at the same time. Since my mom was eight months pregnant, she couldn't walk fast enough for them. I later learned from my brother that they wanted to know if our father had left some money with him. When we arrived at the camp, our fate was to be decided.

For some reason, we were not taken directly to wherever we were going to be killed. The meeting to decide our fate took about an hour. The commander kept going back and forth between us and the leaders of the refugee camp. At that point, we didn't care much about living or dying anymore. Whatever was going to happen was going to happen.

Once it was confirmed that we were to be killed, the leader came back to us. We were seated on the muddy floor with our arms lined up, our legs pushed together, and our hands on our laps.

God and Guns Argument

The commander was screaming at us, but something in my mom's hand caught his attention and created a conversation that helped her be spared that day. She had been holding a Bible since we left the house where we were hiding.

We were Catholics, but my mom had been converted and baptized into the Seventh-day Adventist faith a few months before the war broke out. Since then, she had developed a passion for reading the Bible, and she carried one everywhere she went. She also believed that holding a Bible against her chest would protect us from the killers. That idea made the commander very angry, and he told her that she shouldn't been holding a Bible.

I thought the conversation was irrelevant, but I didn't mind it taking so long since it granted us a few more minutes of life.

The soldier and my mom kept going back and forth about what

they believed. My mom explained that the Bible was her protection, and if he killed her, she was going to go to heaven. She asked, "Why would a person of faith kill innocent children and a pregnant woman who had no part in the country's politics?"

He said it was his duty as a good soldier fighting for his country, which was understandable. He proved that he was a person of faith by showing us the Bible he carried everywhere in the side pocket of his uniform.

I was wondering if my mom's faith or the soldier's faith mattered. We were innocent kids, but we were considered enemies. My mom was not involved in politics at all, and I didn't think God cared about what was going on—and I wasn't even sure if he existed. I wasn't an unbeliever, but I didn't think God was with the soldier who was about to order us killed, or with my mom who had just lost her husband and was about to lose her children, including the one in her womb.

I had heard stories about them cutting open pregnant women and taking out their babies before killing them. I was picturing bullets going through that Bible to my mom's heart and then to us four kids. That was all that was on my mind. We would be lucky because being shot was a privileged death because bullets were expensive. Only the rich died by bullets. Common people died by machetes and bats with nails in them.

Fortunately, none of it went the way I had imagined. The soldier decided to let my mother go, but the children had to stay. I don't know if my mom's faith in holding the Bible worked for her or if the soldier spared her because he felt guilty about killing a fellow believer. All I know is that I was thankful to God that my mom's life was spared that day along with my little sister in her womb. I later learned that she kind of froze and found herself in a flock of people who were fleeing the fighting, and she ended up in a stadium that was guarded by the UN. She gave birth to a little girl after the genocide, and she is still enjoying life. For that, we are thankful.

Unfortunately, the Bible trick did not prevent us from being taken to be killed that day. God sometimes works in mysterious ways; otherwise, I wouldn't be here to write this book.

That soldier and his team decided to let my mom go, but my three siblings and I had to stay. Someone had to pay for what they believed our big brother and the RPF soldiers had done to them. We were kids, but we were considered enemies of the state. Imagine that. However, what was meant to kill you can be used to help you. Help can sometimes come from unexpected places.

An Underground Miracle!

> As long as you are breathing, there is more right with you than wrong with you, no matter what is wrong.
>
> —Jon Kabat-Zinn

The four of us were taken to a nearby hole that was hiding the bodies of the people they were killing at the roadblock. The hole was meant to be a septic tank for a toilet facility that was under construction.

As we were facing death at the edge of that hole, they decided that killing us immediately would not be painful enough. Instead, they decided to hit us with their weapons, push us into the septic tank, and leave us there for seven days to die of hunger. If we were still alive in a week, they would stone us to death.

Imagine listening to this and knowing the end of your life is at hand. The strangest thing is that I did not fear dying. I had accepted the fact that we were powerless—and there was nothing else to do but yield. We were surrounded by a bunch of government-trained soldiers and Interahamwe militia who had been killing people in the weeks since the president's airplane had crashed. Some of them had been killing people before that. The Interahamwe training facility was not far from where we lived, and some of the young people we used to hang out and play soccer with were going there for training.

We always knew we were going to be killed someday, but we didn't know that day was coming so soon. There were rumors that the government and the militia had lists of Tutsis they were planning to massacre, and that was already taking place in different parts of the country.

They threw us all into that septic tank hole. Once I realized they were not going to kill us at that time, I decided to jump into the hole. I ran and jumped right in. I had not been hit yet or wounded, but a soldier threw a shock absorber at me as I was jumping into the hole. It hit my ribs, and I landed in the pit. I could not breathe for a very long time. We used that shock absorber to dig ourselves out of the septic tank hole.

How We Got Out

We were in that septic tank hole for two days. On the third day, it rained so hard that water started gushing through a tiny hole between the bricks. The water started rising up to our waists. We had to lift my little brother and hold him above the water level. We would pass him to another sibling when we became more tired and weak. We were already tired and weak from not eating anything for several days.

As the water kept rising, we were feeling increasingly desperate. We started imagining all of us drowning. Not knowing what else we could do, we turned to a force we thought could be stronger than the rain. We decided to pray. All we needed at that moment was for God to stop the rain. I don't think I knew for sure whether he existed or cared, but in that moment of desperation, he was the only higher power I could turn to. We all took turns and asked God to stop the rain.

A one-line prayer was all we knew:

Please, God, stop the rain.
Please stop the rain.
Please stop the rain.
Please, God, stop the rain.

Whether it was because we prayed or because it was time for the rain to stop on its own, I cannot say. I somehow feel like I can identify with the biblical story where a guy was asked to testify about whether Jesus had opened his eyes by his own power or by the power of darkness, and he replied that all he knew was that he had been blind and now he could see. The argument was about whether Jesus was a holy man of God or not. He decided not to get into their argument since they knew more about the subject than he did. The rain stopped while we prayed, but we can't say for sure if it was because of our prayers. The rain eventually stopped, and we happened to be begging God to intervene and stop it.

The rain did not drown us, and it ended up saving our lives. As it kept pouring down, it softened the dirt beneath the concrete that was above us. As soon as the rain stopped, I climbed to the top and used the shock absorber to dig us out. Once the hole was big enough for our heads and shoulders, we started pushing each other out. We hadn't eaten for days, and we were not going to stay in that hole.

Once we got out, we hid ourselves in a tiny kitchen that was next to the bathroom, and tried to figure out what was going on around us. We could hear shooting and lots of bombs. There were explosions and lightning strikes all over the place. We decided to stay in the kitchen until the shooting stopped. We could not tell what time it was, but once it got dark, we went to find something to eat.

We had survived on water only, but finding food was another problem. There was nobody around, and we had little trust in people at that point. We were right in the middle of a battleground. We walked around for a while, but we did not see any other human beings.

Without knowing how dangerous that place was, walking

around felt good. We felt free, and no one seemed to be around to kill us. It was the first time in a long time that we could walk around without feeling the fear of dying. We weren't sure how long it was going to last, but there was a sense of freedom. We were hungry, but we felt free somehow.

Treated as a Ghost

Despite the feeling of relief and feeling alive again, we were still hungry. The longer we kept looking for food without finding it, the closer we got to dying, especially our little brother. We were all hungry, but his life seemed to be slipping through our fingers in front of our eyes. He was very weak, and he was dehydrated. We found a guava tree and started eating some of its fruit. Our little brother's teeth had gotten so weak because they hadn't been used for some time. He couldn't chew. We tried to encourage him to eat so he could gain some energy, but he said his teeth felt like they were going to fall out. We told him to squeeze the juice out of the fruit, but that didn't help much.

We kept walking from house to house, hoping we would find something to eat. We eventually found a family that had stayed behind. When I told them who I was, they didn't believe me because they had heard what had happened to us. Our neighbors had been told that we had been killed and buried in the septic tank hole. I went through their back door and saw a woman, and called out to her. When I told her my name, she dropped the plates she was holding, and ran off. She was terrified.

She told her husband, and he came outside to figure it out. He asked me how I was, and I repeated what I had told his wife. He was in disbelief, but I told him we needed something to feed our little brother. He brought us tea and said that was all they had, and then he told us to leave before anybody found out we were there. If anybody found us there, they would kill his entire family.

We thanked him for the tea and went on our way.

Meeting the RPF Soldiers

On our way back, we saw RPF soldiers digging shelters. That night, we decided to join them in the morning. We spent the night in the banana fields. Before the sun rose, we marched down to them. A soldier told us to stop and identify ourselves. We stopped and said our names.

When he realized that we were just teenagers and kids, he took us to meet his commander. The commander asked us a few questions about who we were, and if we knew if our parents were still alive. My brothers and my sister needed immediate medical attention for their injuries from the machetes. My injuries were not visible, and I was okay compared to my siblings.

He could see that we were hungry, and he asked us when we had last eaten. One of his soldiers cooked chicken, but we could not handle the meat. He found some soup and bananas that we could eat.

When we regained some strength, the commander asked us what we were going to do since we had survived. I told him that I was going to be a soldier.

He said, "Then you will stay with us."

My siblings were moved to a refugee camp, and I stayed behind. I stayed with them for a few weeks, and the war ended shortly thereafter. We returned to the capital and were joined by his family, after they returned from where they had been living as refugees for more than three decades.

A few months after that, the war was completely over, and I was able to go back to a normal life. I returned to school and rejoined my family.

ACKNOWLEDGMENTS

First, I am grateful to God that I am still here.

Second, I thank my wife, Delice, for loving me, and our four children—Aviella, Abe, Astin, and Amiel—for being a source of joy in our lives.

Third, I thank my mother and siblings for their unconditional love and for being there for me through it all.

Fourth, I want to thank all the people God has placed in my life to help me get this far. I wouldn't have made it this far without you.

Finally, thank you for taking the time to read this book. You are a caring person with a life to live—so go ahead and live it!

ABOUT THE AUTHOR

J. B. Manywa is married, a father of four, and lives in Ohio. He is a volunteer minister by vocation and a software support engineer by trade. He is a graduate of Ohio Christian University with a bachelor of arts degree, and he has an associate's degree in IT.

www.ingramcontent.com/pod-product-compliance
Ingram Content Group UK Ltd.
Pitfield, Milton Keynes, MK11 3LW, UK
UKHW041012120225
455007UK00001B/42

9 798385 024643